SEWING FOR TINY TOTS

SEWING FOR TINY TOTS

Sweet & Simple
Clothes, Toys
& Room Accents

SUSAN
COUSINEAU

LARK/CHAPELLE
A Division of Sterling Publishing Co., Inc.
New York

A Lark/Chapelle Book

Chapelle, Ltd., Inc.
P.O. Box 9255, Ogden, UT 84409
(801) 621-2777
(801) 621-2788 Fax
e-mail: chapelle@chapelleltd.com
Web site: www.chapelleltd.com

Library of Congress Cataloging-in-Publication Data

Cousineau, Susan.
    Sewing for tiny tots : sweet and simple clothes, toys & room accents /
Susan Cousineau. — 1st ed.
        p. cm.
    ISBN 1-60059-028-4 (pbk.)
    1. Infants' clothing. 2. Infants' supplies. I. Title.
    TT637.C69 2007
    745.5—dc22

2006032395

EDITOR:
Kathy Sheldon

ART DIRECTOR:
Dana Irwin

COVER DESIGNER:
Cindy LaBreacht

EDITORIAL ASSISTANCE:
Julie Hale
Delores Gosnell

ASSOCIATE ART DIRECTOR:
Lance Wille

ILLUSTRATOR:
Orrin Lundgren

PHOTOGRAPHER:
John Widman

10 9 8 7 6 5 4 3 2 1

First Edition

Published by Lark Books, A Division of
Sterling Publishing Co., Inc.
387 Park Avenue South, New York, N.Y. 10016

Text © 2007, Susan Cousineau
Photography © 2007, Lark Books
Illustrations © 2007, Lark Books

Distributed in Canada by Sterling Publishing,
c/o Canadian Manda Group, 165 Dufferin Street
Toronto, Ontario, Canada M6K 3H6

Distributed in the United Kingdom by GMC Distribution Services,
Castle Place, 166 High Street, Lewes, East Sussex, England BN7 1XU

Distributed in Australia by Capricorn Link (Australia) Pty Ltd.,
P.O. Box 704, Windsor, NSW 2756 Australia

If you have questions or comments about this book, please contact:
Lark Books, 67 Broadway, Asheville, NC 28801
(828) 253-0467

Manufactured in China

ISBN 13: 978-1-60059-028-3
ISBN 10: 1-60059-028-4

For information about custom editions, special sales, premium and corporate purchases, please
contact Sterling Special Sales Department at 800-805-5489 or specialsales@sterlingpub.com.

Contents

INTRODUCTION 6

BASICS 8

PROJECTS 20

CHAPTER 1:
SWEET DREAMS 20
Designer Nursery and
Bedroom Décor

SWEET DREAMS BUNNY NURSERY
ACCENT AND PILLOW 22

COUNTING SHEEP PILLOW
AND WALL QUILT 26

FROG POND RUG 30

TOOTH FAIRY PILLOW 32

GOODNIGHT MOON CRIB
BLANKET AND MOBILE 34

BEDTIME BUDDIES
CRIB MOBILE 37

SNUGGLE BUG
CRIB BLANKET 40

LULLABY LAMBS (BABY
SLEEPING) DOOR HANGER 42

CHAPTER 2:
CUTIE PIE 44
Stylish Clothing and Accessories

CUTE AS A BUTTON
CRITTER CAP 46

SHABBY CHICK HANGER, T-SHIRT,
BOOTIES, AND SOCKS 48

DESIGNER DENIM BIBS 51

BUSY BEE SLIPPERS 54

FLEECY FRIENDS BIBS 56

SEE YA LATER ALLIGATOR
SCARF AND MITTENS 59

CHIC KITTY PURSE
AND SCARF 62

CHAPTER 3:
GIFTS & GIGGLES 66
Fun and Unique Gift Ideas

CHENILLE SNUGGLE BUNNY
AND MINI QUILT 68

CUPCAKE CUTIE BLANKET,
APRON, AND FAVOR BAGS 72

GIRAFFE CUDDLE BLANKET 78

BATH-TIME BUDDIES HOODED
BATH TOWEL 80

DIRTY DUDS COW
LAUNDRY BAG 82

RUB-A-DUB-DUB BATH BAG 84

CHAPTER 4:
DISCOVER & PLAY 86
Toys for Fun and Active Learning

OCEAN FRIENDS
ACTIVITY MAT 88

JUNGLE FRIENDS PACIFIER PALS,
PUPPETS, AND RATTLE 91

WIGGLY WORM
PLAY PAL 94

RIBBIT FROG
RATTLE 96

BARNYARD
BUDDY BLOCKS 98

POCKET BUNNY
ACTIVITY BLANKET 101

"WHAT'S IN MY POCKET?"
ACTIVITY BOOK 104

SWEET TREATS
COUNTING BOOK 107

CHAPTER 5:
HUGS & HEARTSTRINGS .. 110
Precious Keepsakes and
Memory Crafts

KEEPSAKE BIRTH PILLOW 112

MINI JEAN POCKET PURSE 114

KEEPSAKE MEMORY
QUILT AND PILLOW 116

SPECIAL DELIVERY
TOTE BAGS 120

SPRING BLOSSOM
DIAPER BAG 122

BABY'S FIRST YEAR
SOFT KEEPSAKE BOOK 124

TEMPLATES 127

INDEX 136

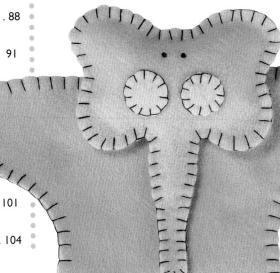

Introduction

Maybe it's the cheerful colors, or perhaps it's the soft fabrics and playful patterns, but one thing is certain: sewing for tots is just plain fun. Instinct seems to make us want to pamper a new arrival, and who can resist making a toddler beam with delight? Sure, you can find things at one of those huge baby stores, but handcrafted creations give you the opportunity to customize colors and design details or add personal touches such as photo transfers, names, and even Baby's footprint to make everyday items special. Whether you're making something for your own child or looking for a gift to give, the time and care that go into a homemade item always make it more meaningful.

Sewing for Tiny Tots offers a multitude of fresh ideas for creating designer-style gifts, clothing ensembles, nursery accents, developmental toys, and enchanting keepsakes. And because that precious new baby won't stay a baby for long, I've included plenty of projects for toddlers in these pages, from unique birthday party items to fun scarves and playful purses.

To get you started, the Basics section provides a general introduction to the tools and materials you'll need, as well as the various crafting techniques you'll use to create the projects in the chapters that follow. Since we all seem to be rushed these days, I've sprinkled in timesaving tips throughout the chapter. And because keeping a baby or toddler safe is always a top priority, I've included safety tips.

Once you're familiar with all of the basics, the creative fun begins! As you skim through the book, you'll discover five chapter themes that include fresh ideas for every aspect of a tot's busy life. The Sweet Dreams chapter has oodles of projects for stitching stylish nursery accents that will make your baby's or child's room adorable. In the clothing and accessories chapter that follows, you'll discover how to transform inexpensive store-bought items into chic wardrobe accessories using our simple embellishing techniques. I'll also show you how to make fun scarves and mittens that a toddler will actually want to wear!

In Gifts & Giggles, you'll find a cuddly giraffe blanket and a chenille snuggle bunny with a matching quilt, fun bath-time projects, and even an adorable cow laundry bag. Need a party idea for your older tot? Our Cupcake Cutie Apron and Favor Bags coordinate perfectly for a cupcake decorating birthday party theme.

Tiny tots love to Discover & Play as they explore the exciting world around them. The toys in this chapter will provide hours of creative playtime, visual stimulation, and developmental learning fun. From "under the sea" activity mats and playtime bunny blankets to jungle critter puppets, rattles, and soft learning toys, these ideas will enhance your child's sensory experiences with lots of giggles along the way.

And last, it's time to get creative with those cherished baby photos. In the final Hugs & Heartstrings chapter, I'll show you how to incorporate your favorite photographs into fabric crafts, clothing accessories, and nursery décor using a simple photo-transferring technique.

No matter which projects you choose to make, remember to have fun. It doesn't matter if every stitch is perfect as long as you're creating with love.

BASICS

This chapter will give you information to help you complete the projects quickly, easily, and successfully. The techniques used to make the items in this book vary from project to project, but they're all quite simple. Some involve hand-stitching and some require machine-stitching or a combination of both.

If you have a fair amount of sewing experience, you may want to skip right to your first project, skim the instructions, make sure you have the necessary materials, see which techniques are required, and then read the section that follows for that particular technique. If you're relatively new to sewing, or you could use a brief refresher, you may instead wish to read this chapter straight through.

BASIC TECHNIQUES

We'll start with the basic techniques I used to make these projects, and then look at tools and materials. The first step (and the one most of us enjoy the most) is choosing your fabric.

Choosing Fabric

The projects in this book use a wide variety of fabrics such as cotton and cotton blend prints, fleece, terry cloth, chenille, and a variety of felts. Of course, you won't always be able to find the exact fabrics in the photos, but you can use my selections as a guide when choosing the fabrics that will put your personal stamp on the projects. When sewing for tiny tots, choose quality fabrics that are soft and durable, especially when creating toys and other items that must stand up to frequent use.

Keep in mind that when yardage requirements are listed, they're based on standard width measurements, such as 44 or 45 inches for cotton prints and 60 inches for fleece. If you choose narrower or wider ones, you may need to purchase more or less fabric. When purchasing felt and wool felt—which are generally sold in a wide range of widths—simply refer to the actual dimensions in the project's materials list to determine your fabric requirements. For the smaller felt projects and appliqué pieces, you can purchase the felt in precut 9 × 12-inch pieces instead of by the yard. If the project is one that will be repeatedly washed, purchase a brand of felt that's machine washable and dryable, and is fade resistant.

Preparing Fabric

Prewash your fabrics before starting, not only to prevent shrinkage, but also to remove harsh chemicals that may irritate Baby's skin. You can skip this step if a project is for decorative use only and won't be laundered. You may prefer to hand-wash your felt (or wash it in a warm/cool gentle cycle) and lay it flat to dry. If you're ever unsure

about the amount of shrinkage or the possibility of the felt's dye bleeding onto another fabric, wash and dry some test pieces first.

Press the fabric before cutting to remove wrinkles and folds. Use steam and a pressing cloth when pressing fabrics such as fleece and felt.

Making Templates

A template is a pattern cut from sturdy material such as template plastic or lightweight cardboard such as poster board. With a template, you can trace the shape onto your fabric quickly and precisely, which ensures more accurate piecing. When making the templates for some of the projects, it may be necessary to enlarge the pattern first on a photocopier. For the larger patterns, it also may be necessary to overlap and tape several pieces together to make a template.

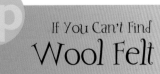

tip

If You Can't Find
Wool Felt

Some of the projects call for wool felt, but if you can't find it easily in your area, you can use regular craft felt instead.

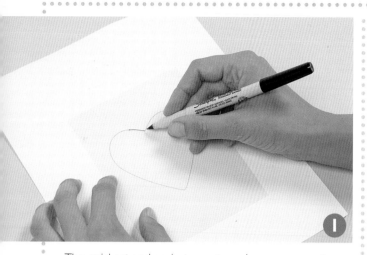

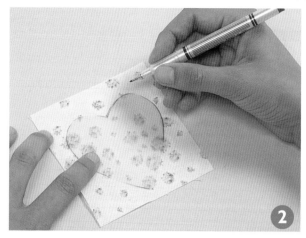

The quickest and easiest way to make a permanent template is to purchase template plastic from your local craft, fabric, or quilt shop. You can use a template-plastic pattern over and over without the edges fraying. Because the plastic is transparent, you can also trace directly over the pattern in one simple step. Simply lay the piece of plastic over your template, trace the shape onto the surface of the plastic with a permanent marker (see photo 1), and use sharp scissors to cut out the shape on the traced lines.

If you don't have template plastic, you can use a lightweight cardboard such as poster board instead. Poster board is available in large sheets that are the perfect size for making the bigger templates in the book. You can cut out the photocopied patterns and trace around them directly onto the cardboard, or use tracing and transfer paper.

Marking Fabric

After you've made your template, use an air-soluble or water-soluble disappearing ink pen to trace around the template and onto your fabric (see photo 2). (For darker fabric, you can use a white dressmaker's or quilter's pencil.) Now you're ready to cut your pieces out.

Cutting Fabric

Cut the pieces from the fabric simply by using a pair of sharp scissors and cutting along the traced pattern lines.

When cutting precise shapes—such as squares, rectangles, triangles, and strips—from fabric, you'll get the best results by using a rotary cutter, a transparent grid-lined ruler, and a rotary-cutting mat (see photo 3).

Before you make that first cut, square up your fabric so that you're working with a straight edge. If your fabric is larger than the mat and ruler, simply fold it in half to double the layers. Place the fabric on the cutting mat with the folded edge aligned on a horizontal grid line and the right edge along a vertical grid line. Then place the ruler onto the fabric so that it lines up with the grid lines on the cutting mat. Hold the ruler firmly in place with one hand, then use the rotary cutter to trim away the excess fabric along the vertical edge. See the tip box for more on using a rotary cutter.

SEAM ALLOWANCES

■ *As a general rule of thumb, the majority of sewing projects in this book use a ¼-inch seam allowance (with the exception of the pillow covers, which use a ½-inch seam allowance). However, when using stretchy fabrics such as fleece, I sometimes use a slightly larger seam allowance, anywhere from ⅜ to ½ inch.*

■ *All template patterns include any necessary seam allowances (they're indicated by dotted lines on the outer edges).*

■ *When piecing, press the seam allowances to one side, usually toward the darker fabric.*

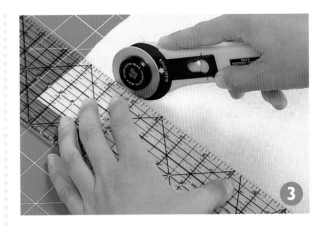

Using a Rotary Cutter

• **Hold the rotary cutter at a 45° angle, making sure the blade is placed firmly against the outer edge of the ruler.**

• **Maintain an even pressure on the rotary cutter while cutting, and always cut away from yourself for maximum control and safety.**

• **Always keep the guard over the blade when you're not cutting.**

Basting

Basting is the technique used to temporarily adhere fabric pieces together. Although there are numerous ways to baste fabric pieces and cutouts onto your designs, I prefer to use a fabric spray adhesive. (Other basting options include fabric glue sticks and straight pins.) To use the fabric adhesive, simply spray a thin, even layer onto the back of the fabric piece to be adhered. For the quilt projects, you'll want to spray the batting as well. As with all commercial products, be sure to refer to the manufacturer's instructions, since they may vary from brand to brand.

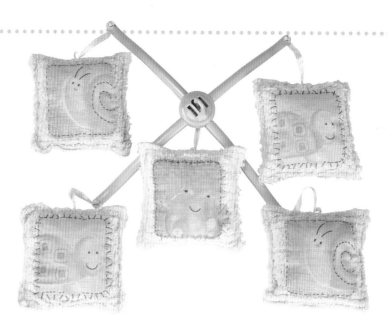

When basting, keep in mind that the dotted lines on the template patterns indicate the overlap of fabric pieces. You can use these lines as a reference when layering your fabric motifs.

Piecing a Quilt or Blanket

When sewing fabric squares together to create a quilt or blanket, pin the first two squares together, right sides facing, then stitch along the right edge using the desired seam allowance. (Be sure to lay out your block pattern so that the pieces are sewn in the proper order.) Additional squares are added to each row in the same manner. When each row of blocks is complete, pin and sew the rows together in the same fashion. Press seam allowances as you go to ensure more accurate piecing.

Fusible Web Appliqué

A number of the projects in the book use fusible web to make decorative appliqués. Of the many appliqué products available, I find paper-backed fusible webs to be the quickest and simplest to use. Fusible webs melt between two layers of fabric when ironed to create an instant bond. Fabrics that are 100 percent cotton tend to be the easiest to use with this technique.

You can purchase individually packaged sheets of fusible web or buy it by the yard. Unless otherwise specified in the materials list, the projects in this book use a light or regular-weight fusible web. The regular-weight fusible webs have a lighter coating of adhesive, allowing you to machine-stitch or embroider after fusing. Use heavy-weight fusible webs (or brands with an "ultra-hold") for no-sew appliqué projects. There are many different brands of fusible webs available, and the techniques for each vary, so it's important to follow the manufacturer's instructions for your particular brand. What follows in the steps and tip box are the most common techniques for making a fusible web appliqué.

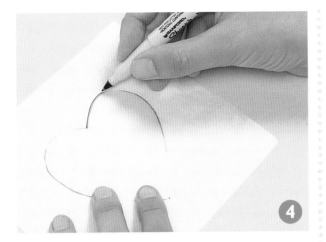

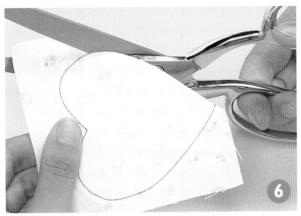

Making a Fusible Web Appliqué

1. Trace the template shape onto the paper side of a piece of fusible web using a fabric or permanent marking pen. (See photo 4.) (Remember to reverse the templates for nonsymmetrical shapes.)

2. Using sharp scissors, cut around the shape, cutting slightly larger (by about ¼ inch) than the traced design.

3. Iron the cutout, paper side up, onto the wrong side of the fabric. (See photo 5.)

4. Cut out the appliqué on the traced lines. (See photo 6.)

5. Peel away the paper backing, then iron the appliqué onto the background fabric. (See photo 7.)

tip

Quick Appliqué

For a quick and easy appliqué technique, you can apply the fusible web onto a piece of fabric first, then trace and cut out the desired template shape directly from the fused fabric. This technique also works best with simple block appliqués (Counting Sheep Wall Quilt, page 26) or preprinted appliqué designs (such as the Bedtime Buddies Mobile, page 37).

Basic Embroidery Techniques

The projects in this book will give you a wonderful introduction to basic embroidery techniques. If you've never embroidered before, take some time to review this section, particularly the Stitch Guide (on the following page) for illustrations featuring the simple stitches used in this book.

As you glance through the project instructions, you'll notice that each embroidery stitch has its own unique function. For example, blanket and straight stitches are used to sew around pillows, blankets, and appliqué pieces. French knots are perfect for eyes, and lazy daisy stitches create charming leaves and flower petals. Backstitches, satin stitches, and running stitches are commonly used to stitch pattern designs such as mouths,

noses, lettering, and a variety of decorative details. Before stitching these pattern motifs, you'll need to transfer the design onto your fabric.

Transferring the Embroidery Design

Since most of the embroidered designs used in this book are very basic (facial features, lettering, etc.), I prefer to use the direct transfer method to transfer a design onto the fabric. This is simply a matter of drawing the design directly onto the fabric using a disappearing ink (air-soluble or water-soluble) marking pen. You can freehand the stitching lines; if you make a mistake, use a damp sponge to gently wipe away any unwanted lines and redraw the design.

STITCH GUIDE

Follow the stitch illustrations to bring the needle up at odd numbers and down at even numbers.

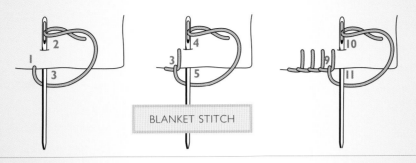

BLANKET STITCH

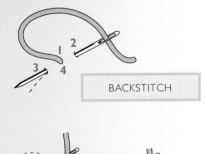

BACKSTITCH

SINGLE CROSS STITCH

FRENCH KNOTS

SATIN STITCH

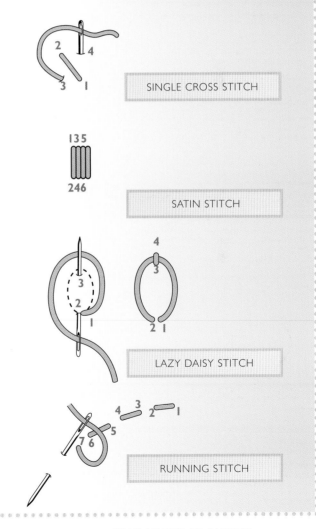

LAZY DAISY STITCH

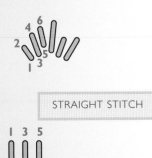

STRAIGHT STITCH

WHIPSTITCH

RUNNING STITCH

Using Photo Transfers

Several of the projects in this book feature photo transfers. Here are a few helpful hints for transferring your favorite photos onto fabric:

- Remember to use your printer or image software settings to flip the image before printing the photo onto your transfer paper. If you don't flip the image, it will print backwards when ironed onto your fabric.

- If you don't have a scanner or digital camera, you can have your regular print film

burned onto a disc or CD at your local photo-processing center. Or visit your local copy or print shop to make digital images of your photos. You can also ask a friend to email you a digital image.

- Be sure to read the manufacturer's instructions for your brand of photo transfer paper before beginning your project.

BASIC MATERIALS, TOOLS, AND EQUIPMENT

The projects in this book require the materials and tools anyone who sews is likely to have on hand. Below is a list of the general supplies you'll need. Since most of the projects call for these same basic necessities, they'll be listed here instead of repeating them in the "What You Need" list at the start of each project.

Tools

Scissors. For cutting fabric, always use a pair of sharp, high-quality scissors. To maintain the sharpness and quality of your scissors, use a different pair for cutting trims and heavier materials such as template plastic or poster board.

Pinking shears. These add a quick, decorative edge to your fabric pieces.

Access to a photocopier. Use a home or commercial photocopier to reproduce and enlarge patterns as necessary.

Transparent acrylic grid-lined ruler, rotary cutter, and rotary-cutting mat. Use to cut precise shapes such as squares, rectangles, triangles, and long strips more quickly and accurately. (See page 11 for cutting tips.)

Iron. A general household iron is another basic necessity for most sewing projects. It's used for pressing fabrics and seams, for fusible web appliqué, and for transferring photos onto fabric.

Measuring tape. An essential tool for measuring fabric pieces and trims.

Permanent marker, pencil or pen. Permanent markers work well when tracing template shapes onto plastic. If you're tracing template shapes onto cardboard instead, you can use a pencil or pen.

Disappearing-ink marking pen. An air-soluble or water-soluble disappearing-ink pen can be used to trace template shapes onto fabric and to transfer pattern details for hand-stitching and embroidery. If the fabric is too dark to see the traced lines of the marking pen, use a white dressmaker's or quilter's pencil instead.

Sewing machine. A must for all the machine-stitched projects.

Hand-sewing and embroidery needles. You'll need general-purpose needles for hand-sewing and for stitching trims and embellishments. Crewel needles are a good choice for most embroidery techniques. Use heavier, extra-long needles such as darners when stitching through tougher materials such as the Frog Pond Rug (page 30).

tip Quick Circles

You can use plastic thread spools, cardboard ribbon spools, or spray can caps as quick and easy "ready-made" templates for some of the smaller circle shapes used in this book for eyes, noses, cheeks, etc. You can also purchase plastic circle templates at art and office supply stores.

Materials

Fabric. You'll use a wide variety of fabrics to create the projects in this book; fabrics are specified in the individual project lists. For further information, refer to the Choosing Fabric section on page 9.

Template plastic or poster board. Use these to make templates for your projects. You'll also need tracing paper and transfer paper for tracing smaller projects onto poster board.

Fabric spray adhesive. Use to baste fabric pieces for sewing and embroidery. Fabric basting glue sticks are a popular alternative to the sprays.

SAFETY FIRST!

Small trims and embellishments can present a choking hazard for babies and small tots. This may not be a concern if the project is for decorative purposes only and is displayed out of reach of the child. However, as a precautionary safety measure, it's best to use a heavy-duty thread and test all trims by pulling on them as hard as you can. Another creative safety option is to use dental floss to stitch the trims and embellishments. Since hand-stitching is perfectly safe, you may opt to use decorative embroidery stitches to embellish the entire project, thereby eliminating the trims altogether. For example, use a French knot or satin stitch instead of a button to make a nose, and use lazy daisy stitches to create a flower instead of using a flower trim.

Straight pins. A necessity for most sewing projects for piecing, basting, etc.

Threads. Use basic all-purpose polyester thread for most machine sewing. For the wall quilt projects, you may prefer to use 100 percent cotton quilting thread. To make trims extra secure, use the stronger threads made for hand-quilting and upholstery instead of regular sewing threads. Invisible nylon thread is a great alternative to use for stitching trims and adding extra security to iron-on appliqués.

Cotton embroidery floss. A necessity for all embroidered projects. Refer to the individual project instructions for the required colors and the number of strands.

Fusible web. Use light or regular-weight fusible web unless otherwise specified in the project's

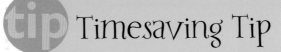

Timesaving Tip

To save time, you can always use your sewing machine to stitch around appliqué pieces, blankets, etc., instead of using the hand-stitched embroidery techniques suggested. Most modern sewing machines offer a diverse range of stitching options to give a decorative hand-stitched look to your appliqué designs.

materials list. The regular-weight fusible web has a lighter coat of adhesive that enables you to machine-stitch or embroider around the appliqué after fusing. Heavyweight (no-sew) or ultra-hold fusible web has a heavier bonding agent that secures the appliqué pieces without sewing.

CHAPTER ONE

Sweet Dreams

DESIGNER NURSERY AND BEDROOM DÉCOR

After Baby's arrival, the nursery

is sure to be the busiest—

and happiest—

room in the house. Regardless of the theme and color

palette you choose for the nursery, you'll want to create

a space that reflects your personal taste and style, as well

as the love you feel for your child. In this chapter, we've

included everything you need to decorate that special

room. From enchanting bunnies and whimsical sheep, to

a magical moonlit night, you're sure to find plenty of

inspiration for pampering your

baby in

happily-ever-after

comfort and style.

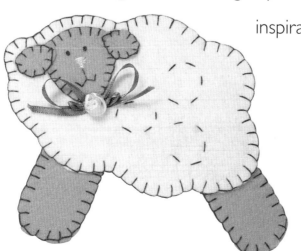

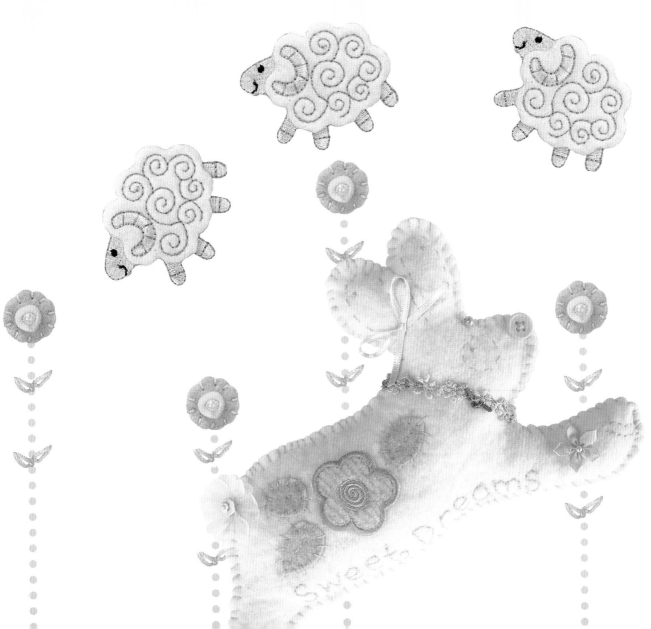

Sweet Dreams Bunny Nursery Accent and Pillow

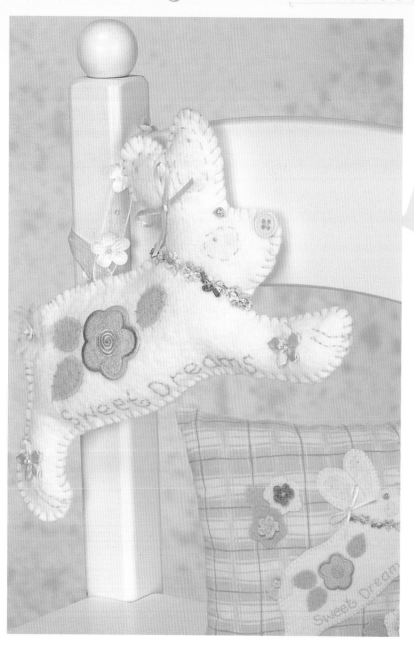

A

Add a *sweet touch* to the nursery with this enchanting bunny accent and pillow. Hang the bunny on a doorknob as a reminder that Baby is napping, or let it hop anywhere the nursery could use a playful touch of fun. On the pillow, the same playful bunny frolics through the flower blossoms, chasing her fluttering friend.

To make the nursery accent:

WHAT YOU NEED

Basic materials, tools, and equipment (page 17)

Bunny and small leaf templates (page 127)

2 pieces of cream wool felt, each $10\frac{1}{2}$ x 8 inches

Pink flower iron-on appliqué, $1\frac{1}{2}$ inches

Scraps of wool felt in pale green

Cotton embroidery floss in pink and beige

Pale pink acrylic paint (or you can use pink powdered blush)

Small stencil or deerfoot brush (or you can use a cotton swab)

Pink pearl bead, 6 mm diameter

$2\frac{3}{4}$ inches of pink and green lace flower trim, $\frac{3}{8}$ inch wide

9 inches of pink ribbon, $\frac{1}{8}$ inch wide

2 pink ribbon flowers with pearl centers, each $\frac{3}{4}$ inch

10 inches of pale green ribbon with pink flower accents, $\frac{1}{2}$ inch wide

Polyester fiberfill

Pink button

Sheer pink ribbon flower, $1\frac{1}{4}$ inches

WHAT YOU DO

1. Use the bunny template on page 127 to trace and cut out two bunny shapes from the two pieces of cream felt.

2. Iron the flower appliqué onto the front center of one of the felt bunny pieces. For extra security, you can add a few stitches using matching or invisible thread.

3. Use the small leaf template on page 127 to trace and cut out three leaf shapes from the pale green felt.

4. Referring to the template or photo for placement, baste the three felt leaves onto the bunny, with two leaves on the left, and the remaining leaf on the right side of the flower appliqué.

5. Straight stitch around the leaves using two strands of the beige floss, then add a running stitch along the center of each leaf.

6. Trace the phrase "Sweet Dreams" along the bottom edge of

the bunny, then backstitch each word using three strands of the pink floss.

7. Using two strands of the beige floss, backstitch a line in between the ears, then backstitch two lines onto each paw.

8. Using two strands of the pink floss, outline the inner ears and a small circle for the cheek with a running stitch. Very sparingly dry-brush the inner ears and cheek with pink acrylic paint using a small stencil or deerfoot brush. (You can instead use a cotton swab to apply just a bit of pink powdered blush to these spots.)

9. Using the beige floss, stitch French knot accents onto the inner ears and cheeks.

10. Stitch the pink bead on for the eye, then stitch the lace flower trim onto the neck. Tie a bow with the ⅛-inch-wide pink ribbon, then stitch the bow onto the ear, and the two pink ribbon flower trims onto each leg.

11. Stitch the ends of the 10-inch ribbon piece onto the back of the bunny as a hanger.

12. With the edges aligned, place the two bunny pieces wrong sides together (the ribbon hanger will be sandwiched between the two layers). Whipstitch (or blanket-stitch) around the bunny using two strands of the beige floss, leaving an opening wide enough at the bottom for stuffing.

13. Stuff the bunny with polyester fiberfill, then stitch the opening closed.

14. Stitch the pink button on for the nose, then add the sheer flower trim for the tail.

To make the pillow:

WHAT YOU NEED

Basic materials, tools, and equipment (page 17)

½ yard of pink and cream print fabric

Bunny, flower, small and large leaf templates (page 127)

Piece of cream wool felt, 10½ x 8 inches

1½-inch pink flower iron-on appliqué

Scraps of wool felt in pale green, cream, and pink

Cotton embroidery floss in beige and pink

Pale pink acrylic paint (or you can use pink powdered blush)

Small stencil or deerfoot brush (or you can use a cotton swab)

Pink pearl bead, 6 mm diameter

2¾ inches of pink and green lace flower trim, ⅜ inch wide

9 inches of pink ribbon, ⅛ inch wide

2 pink ribbon flowers with pearl centers, each ¾ inch

Pink button

1¼-inch sheer pink ribbon flower

5 chenille flowers, each ¾ inch (I use 2 fuchsia, 2 pink, and 1 cream.)

Pink dragonfly iron-on appliqué, 2 inches wide

Pillow form, 14 x 14 inches (or polyester fiberfill)

WHAT YOU DO

1. Cut two 14½-inch-square pieces of the pink and cream print fabric.

2. Use the bunny template on page 127 to trace and cut out one bunny shape from the cream felt.

3. Baste the felt bunny piece at a 45° angle onto the center of one of the 14½-inch fabric squares, then whipstitch (or blanket-stitch) around the bunny.

4. Refer to steps 2 through 10 on pages 23 and 24 to add the flower appliqué, felt leaves, trims, and decorative stitching onto the bunny. Then stitch the pink button on for the nose and add the sheer flower trim for the tail.

5. Use the flower and large leaf templates on page 127 to trace and cut out two flowers from the cream felt, three flowers from the pink felt, and three large leaves from the pale green felt.

6. Referring to the photo for placement, baste the felt leaves and flowers in a pleasing arrangement onto the pillow cover, then straight stitch around the edges of the leaves and flowers using two strands of the beige floss. Add a running stitch along the center of each leaf.

7. Stitch the chenille flowers onto the centers of the felt flowers.

8. Stitch the dragonfly appliqué onto the top right corner, then backstitch the decorative stitches from the bunny's nose to the dragonfly using two strands of the beige floss.

9. With the edges aligned, pin the two fabric squares right sides together. Using a ½-inch seam allowance, sew the squares together leaving an opening wide enough at the bottom to insert the pillow form.

10. Trim the corners, turn the pillow right side out, and insert the pillow form (or stuff the entire pillow with polyester fiberfill). Then slip stitch the opening closed.

Counting Sheep Pillow and Wall Quilt

Decorating a nursery can present a challenge for those parents-to-be who prefer to wait until the big day to discover their baby's gender. As a fresh alternative to the traditional pink or blue baby theme, this exquisite lamb wall quilt and coordinating pillow are designed in neutral shades of cream and green to welcome any baby in style.

To make the pillow:

WHAT YOU NEED

Basic materials, tools, and equipment (page 17)

Sheep template (page 127)

Scraps of cream and tan felt or wool felt

Piece of green print fabric, 8 inches square

Cotton embroidery floss in dark brown and pale pink

9 inches of dark green ribbon, ⅛ inch wide

Ivory ribbon rosebud with flat green bow, 1 inch wide

2 pieces of cream chenille fabric, each 14½ x 14½ inches

32 inches of jumbo pale green chenille rickrack

4 pieces of pale green ribbon, each ⅛ x 9 inches

4 ivory ribbon rosebuds with green leaves, each 1¼-inches wide

Pillow form, 14 x 14 inches (or polyester fiberfill)

WHAT YOU DO

1. Use the sheep template on page 127 to trace and cut out one sheep body shape from the cream felt and one face shape, two ear shapes, and two leg shapes from the tan felt.

2. Baste and stitch the sheep motif onto the center of the green print square (see Counting Sheep Wall Quilt instructions, page 28).

3. Tie a bow with the dark green ribbon, then stitch it and the 1-inch ivory ribbon rosebud onto the neck of the sheep.

4. Baste the sheep square onto the center of one of the 14½-inch chenille squares, and stitch around the edges of the sheep square to secure it. Then stitch the piece of pale green chenille rickrack around the edges of the sheep square.

5. Tie four bows with the pale green ribbon, then stitch them and the four 1¼-inch ivory ribbon rosebuds onto the corners of the sheep square.

6. With the edges aligned, pin the two chenille squares right sides together. Using a ½-inch seam allowance, sew the squares together leaving an opening wide enough at the bottom to insert the pillow form. Trim the corners, then turn the piece right side out.

7. Insert the pillow form (or stuff the pillow with polyester fiberfill), then slip stitch the opening closed.

Wall Quilt

WHAT YOU NEED

Basic materials, tools, and equipment (page 17)

⅝ yard of pale green gingham print fabric

⅓ yard of cream chenille fabric

Sheep and number templates (page 127)

Scraps of felt or wool felt in cream, tan, and pale green

Cotton embroidery floss in dark brown and pale pink

5 pieces of dark green ribbon, each ⅛ x 9 inches

5 ivory ribbon rosebuds with flat green bows, each 1 inch wide

Fusible web

Scraps of assorted green print fabrics

4 ivory flower buttons

⅓ yard of dark green print fabric (for the border)

1 yard of coordinating green print fabric (for the backing)

Piece of quilt batting, 32 inches square

⅓ yard of pale green print fabric (for the binding)

2 plastic rings (for hanging)

WHAT YOU DO

1. Cut five 9-inch squares out of the pale green gingham print fabric and four 9-inch squares out of the cream chenille fabric.

2. Use the sheep template on page 127 to trace and cut out five sheep body shapes from the cream felt, and five face shapes, 10 ear shapes, and 10 leg shapes from the tan felt.

3. Use the number templates on page 127 to trace and cut out the five number shapes from the pale green felt.

4. Referring to the photo and template for placement, baste the sheep and number shapes onto the five green gingham print squares. Be sure to baste the legs of the sheep first, then position the body to overlap the top seams of the legs. Also, when placing the sheep and number motifs onto each square, remember to allow enough space for the seam allowances along the edges. Continue to baste the felt sheep faces and ears onto the five felt body shapes.

5. Blanket-stitch around the sheep and number shapes using two strands of the dark brown floss. Continue to blanket-stitch around the faces and ears. Satin stitch the noses using three strands of the pale pink floss. Backstitch each mouth with two strands of the brown floss, and add brown French knots for eyes. Add the decorative swirls onto the body shapes using a running stitch and two strands of the brown floss.

6. Tie five small bows with the pieces of dark green ribbon, then stitch a bow and an ivory ribbon rosebud onto the neck of each sheep.

7. Apply the fusible web to the assorted scraps of green print fabrics (see Fusible Web Appliqué, page 12). Then use pinking shears to cut out eight 2½-inch squares. Fuse two of the green print squares onto each of the four larger chenille squares, overlapping them as desired. Straight stitch around the fabric squares, using two strands of the dark brown floss.

8. Stitch an ivory flower button onto the center of the fabric patches.

9. Refer to the Piecing a Quilt section on page 12, then sew the first row of the quilt together so that the first and second sheep squares are on the left and right sides, and one of the chenille squares is in the center. Sew the second row with the third sheep square in the center and a chenille square on each side. Then sew the final row in the same manner as the first, with the fourth and fifth sheep squares on the left and right sides and the remaining chenille square in the center.

10. With the seams aligned, sew the first and second rows together, then sew the final row to

complete the center block.

11. Measure the length of the quilt top through the center, raw edge to raw edge, then use this measurement to cut two 2¼-inch-wide border strips from the dark green print fabric. Pin the border strips onto each side of the quilt top, then sew them.

12. Measure the width of the quilt top through the center, raw edge to raw edge, then use this measurement to cut two additional 2¼-inch-wide border strips from the dark green print fabric. Sew these strips onto the top and bottom of the quilt top in the same manner as the side borders.

13. Cut the quilt batting and backing fabric to a size that's slightly larger than that of the quilt top. Then baste the batting in between the top and bottom layers of the quilt with the wrong sides of the quilt top and backing facing together.

14. Pin the three layers together, stitch-in-the-ditch along the seams, then trim the backing and batting even with the edges of the quilt top.

15. Finish the edges of the quilt with the pale green print, using your preferred binding technique. Then stitch two plastic rings onto the back of the quilt for hanging.

Frog Pond Rug

You'll make a big splash with this delightful frog pond rug. What a fun way to encourage your tot to hop into the tub. The rug is super-easy to make using an inexpensive blue plush bath mat and some scraps of colorful felt. Use the frog theme as inspiration to decorate the room with all sorts of bright and cheerful frog, bug, and lily pad accessories.

WHAT YOU NEED

Basic materials, tools, and equipment (page 17)

Darning needle

Frog, lily pad, and flower template (page 129)

Piece of lime green felt, 10 x 12 inches

Scraps of felt in dark green, yellow, cream, and black

Black cotton embroidery floss

Blue plush nylon bath mat, 24 x 17 inches (Note: A soft rug is needed in order to stitch through the bottom.)

WHAT YOU DO

1. Using the template on page 129, trace and cut out one frog from the lime green felt. Then cut out one lily pad from the dark green felt, three spots and a circular flower center from the yellow felt, two circular eyes and a flower from the cream felt, and two inner eye circles from the black felt.

2. Baste the two cream circles onto the frog for the eyes, referring to the template or photo for placement. Then blanket-stitch around the eyes, using two strands of the black floss. Baste the two inner black circles onto the eyes, and use a straight stitch around the edges to secure them.

3. Trace the mouth, then back-stitch it using two strands of the black floss. Add a French knot at each end of the mouth.

4. Satin stitch the two nostrils using two strands of the black floss.

5. Baste the three yellow spots onto the frog, then blanket-stitch around the spots using two strands of the black floss.

6. Baste the circular yellow center onto the flower, then blanket-stitch around the circle using two strands of the black floss.

7. Baste the lily pad onto the center of the rug about three inches from the bottom, then blanket-stitch around it with three strands of the black floss.

8. Baste the frog onto the center of the lily pad, then blanket-stitch around the frog using three strands of the black floss.

9. Baste the flower onto the left side of the lily pad so that it slightly overlaps the bottom of the frog, then blanket-stitch around the flower using three strands of the black floss.

Tooth Fairy Pillow

If there's an older tot in the house, he or she *will* certainly appreciate being the focus of attention, too. Make a child's first visit from the tooth fairy extra-memorable with this charming keepsake pillow. The smiling tooth motif plays double duty as a clever pocket to hold any surprises left in the night. With a ribbon for hanging, the pillow makes a darling accent to dress up a doorknob or bedpost.

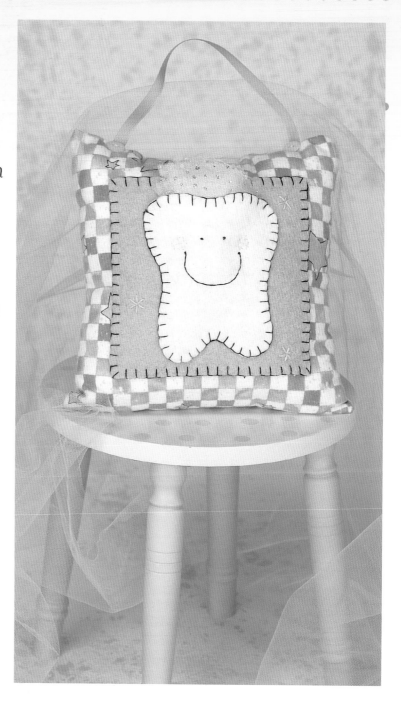

WHAT YOU NEED

Basic materials, tools, and equipment (page 17)

Tooth template (page 127)

Scrap of white or cream wool felt

Cotton embroidery floss in black, yellow, and pale pink

Piece of blue wool felt, 6 x 6 inches

2 pieces of blue-and-white checkered flannel (or cotton) print fabric, each 10 x 10 inches

Polyester fiberfill

10 inches of blue ribbon, ³/₈ inch wide

2 yellow buttons

WHAT YOU DO

1. Trace and cut out the tooth shape on page 127 from the white or cream felt.

2. Trace the mouth onto the felt tooth shape, then backstitch the mouth using two strands of the black floss. Use the black floss to add a black French knot at each end of the mouth.

3. Stitch two French knots for the eyes using two strands of the black floss. Straight stitch the cheek accents with two strands of the pink floss.

4. Use two strands of the black floss to blanket-stitch along the top edge of the tooth. This is where the tooth pocket will remain open.

Then pin the tooth shape onto the center of the 6-inch piece of blue felt. Using two strands of the black floss, complete the blanket stitch along the outer edge of the tooth so that the stitches join the ones already in place at the top opening.

5. Referring to the photo or pattern for placement, straight stitch the three star accents onto the blue felt using six strands of the yellow floss.

6. Baste the tooth square onto the center of one of the 10-inch fabric squares, then blanket-stitch around the square using two strands of the black floss.

7. With the edges aligned, pin the two 10-inch-square pieces right sides together. Using a ¼-inch seam allowance, sew along the edges of the square, leaving an opening wide enough at the bottom for stuffing. Trim the corners, then turn the piece right side out.

8. Stuff the pillow with polyester fiberfill, then slip stitch the opening closed.

9. Stitch the ends of the blue ribbon onto the top sides of the pillow for a hanger, then stitch a yellow button onto each end of the ribbon hanger.

Goodnight Moon Crib Blanket and Mobile

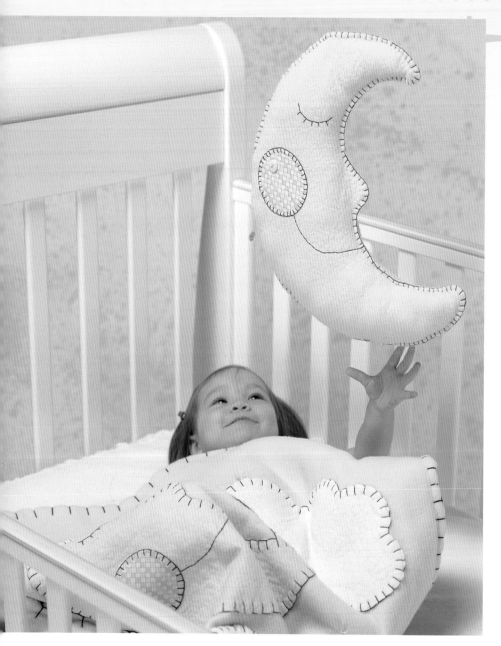

Transform your nursery into a moonlit wonderland with this enchanting crib blanket and sleeping moon mobile. Stitched entirely by hand, the cuddly fleece blanket will lull Baby into dreamland. Complete the theme by hanging the moon pillow above the crib with invisible nylon thread—the moon will look as though it's floating magically in the sky.

To make the blanket:

WHAT YOU NEED

Basic materials, tools, and equipment (page 17)

Moon and cloud templates (page 128)

Piece of yellow wool felt, 15 x 17 inches

Fusible web

Scrap of pink print fabric

Pale blue button

Cotton embroidery floss in black and yellow

3 pieces of white or cream wool felt, each 13 x 10 inches

2 pieces of pale blue fleece, each 28 x 35 inches

WHAT YOU DO

1. Trace and cut out the moon template on page 128 from the yellow felt.

2. Apply the fusible web onto the pink print fabric, then trace and cut out a 3¼-inch circle (see Fusible Web Appliqué, page 12). Fuse the fabric circle onto the felt moon shape for the cheek, referring to the template or photo for placement.

3. Stitch the blue button onto the cheek.

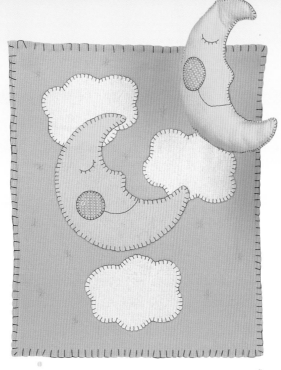

4. Blanket-stitch around the cheek, using two strands of the black floss.

5. Trace the mouth and eye onto the moon, then backstitch them using two strands of the black floss.

6. Use the cloud template on page 128 to trace and cut out three cloud shapes from the white or cream felt. Then baste the three cloud shapes onto one of the blue fleece blanket pieces, referring to the photo for placement.

7. Baste the moon at a bit of an angle so that it slightly overlaps the two cloud shapes.

8. Blanket-stitch around the moon and three clouds, using two strands of the black floss.

9. Randomly straight stitch several star shapes, using six strands of the yellow floss.

10. With the edges aligned, pin the two blanket pieces wrong sides together, then blanket-stitch around the edges of the piece with six strands of the black floss.

Safety Note: We couldn't help putting this adorable tot who was fascinated by the moon mobile into our crib for the photo. But mobiles are meant for visual stimulation and decorative purposes only and should be removed once the child has reached about five months of age or starts to grab for things. At this time, you can mount the moon in a location that's out of the child's reach or use it as a decorative pillow.

WHAT YOU NEED

Basic materials, tools, and equipment (page 17)

Moon template (page 128)

2 pieces of yellow wool felt, each 15 x 17 inches

Fusible web

Scraps of pink print fabric

2 pale blue buttons

Black cotton embroidery floss

Polyester fiberfill

Invisible thread (for hanging)

WHAT YOU DO

1. Use the template on page 128 to trace and cut out two moon shapes from the pieces of yellow felt.

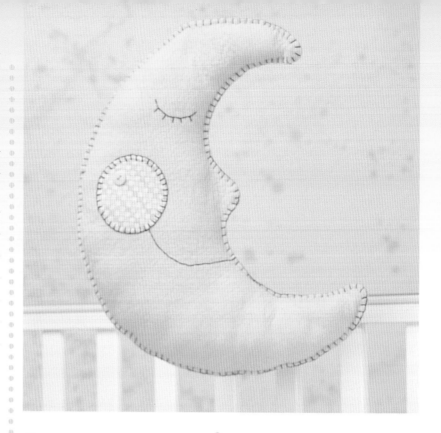

tip

Starry, Starry Night

Add to this theme by painting the moon and cloud shapes onto the nursery ceiling, then adding press-on glow-in-the-dark stars that will twinkle in the night.

2. Apply the fusible web onto the pink print fabric, then trace and cut out two 3¼-inch circles (see Fusible Web Appliqué, page 12). Referring to the template or photo for placement, fuse the two fabric circles onto the felt moon shapes for the cheeks. Important: Remember that the back side of the moon will be done in reverse so that both sides will face outwards when pieced together.

3. Stitch the blue buttons onto the cheeks.

4. Blanket-stitch around the cheeks using two strands of the black floss.

5. Trace the mouth and eye onto each moon shape with the backside in reverse, then backstitch them using two strands of the black floss.

6. With the edges aligned, place the two moon shapes wrong sides together and blanket-stitch around the edges, using two strands of the black floss. Be sure to leave an opening in the center that's wide enough for stuffing.

7. Stuff the moon with polyester fiberfill, then blanket-stitch the opening closed.

8. Stitch a piece of invisible thread to the top of the moon shape, and hang as desired.

Bedtime Buddies Crib Mobile

In addition to a charming nursery accent, a crib mobile offers visual stimulation for babies at their earliest stages of development. This quick and easy mobile consists of miniature chenille pillows embellished with cute critter appliqués. I chose turtle, frog, and snail images, but with the endless variety of fabrics available, you'll have no problem finding a design to complement your nursery decor.

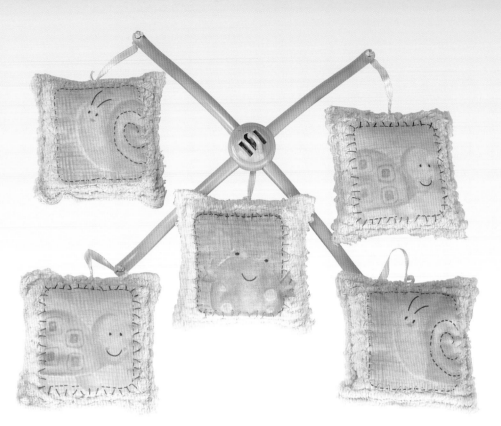

WHAT YOU NEED

Basic materials, tools, and equipment (page 17)

Scraps of chenille fabric in coordinating colors, enough to cut ten 4½-inch squares (I use pink, blue, and cream.)

Fusible web

Print fabric with ten 3-inch critter or bug motifs (or motif to fit your nursery)

Coordinating cotton embroidery floss

Polyester fiberfill

40 inches of ivory ribbon, ¼ inch wide

Sewing needle with large eye

Crib mobile attachment (The one I use holds knotted ribbon hangers.)

WHAT YOU DO

1. Cut the chenille fabric into ten 4½-inch squares. (I cut four squares from the pink chenille, four from the blue chenille, and two from the cream chenille.)

2. Apply the fusible web onto the print fabric, then cut out 10 of the critter or bug images so that they're approximately 3 inches square (see Fusible Web Appliqué, page 12). Fuse the 10 motifs onto the centers of the 10 chenille squares.

3. Straight stitch around the motifs using two strands of the coordinating floss. (I use blue floss on the pink chenille, yellow floss on the blue chenille, and pink floss on the cream chenille.)

4. With the edges aligned and colors matching, pin two of the 10 chenille squares wrong sides together. Continue to pin the remaining eight squares together to piece a total of five miniature pillows.

5. Using a ¼-inch seam allowance, sew the chenille squares together, leaving an opening wide enough at the bottom for stuffing. (I add the ribbon hangers in step 8, after the pillows are sewn. However, you may prefer to cut and sandwich the ribbon pieces into the top of each pillow and stitch them in during this step.)

6. Stuff the pillows with polyester fiberfill. Then slip stitch the bottom openings on each pillow closed.

7. For the ribbon hangers, cut five 8-inch pieces of the ivory ribbon.

8. For each pillow, thread the end of the ribbon piece into the needle, then insert the needle into the top center of the pillow and tie a knot at one end to secure it. (You can ignore this step if you've already sewn the ribbon piece into the pillow in step 5.)

9. Knot the top of each ribbon piece so that the hangers are approximately 3 inches long. (For contrast, I use a shorter length that's about 2 inches long for the center pillow.) Trim the excess ribbon at the top and bottom knots.

10. Insert the ribbon hangers into the mobile arm attachment.

Safety Note: Be sure to read the manufacturer's instructions for safely mounting the mobile attachment onto the crib, and see the safety note on page 35. You can also disassemble the mobile and use the miniature pillows as decorative accents.

Snuggle Bug Crib Blanket

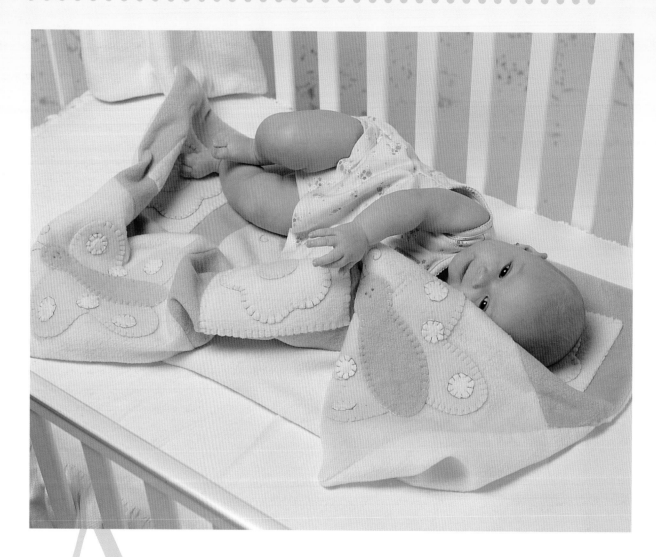

Add a touch of springtime whimsy to the nursery with this cheery blanket. For a charming variation, use the cuddly fleece fabrics to make a coordinating butterfly or blossom block pillow.

WHAT YOU NEED

Basic materials, tools, and equipment (page 17)

Butterfly and flower templates (page 128)

⅜ yard of pink fleece

⅜ yard of pale purple fleece

¾ yard of cream fleece

¼ yard of yellow fleece

Cotton embroidery floss in yellow, pink, and pale purple

WHAT YOU DO

1. Cut three 12-inch squares from the piece of pink fleece, three 12-inch squares from the piece of purple fleece, and three 7-inch squares from the piece of cream fleece.

2. Use the butterfly template on page 128 to trace and cut out three wing shapes from the yellow fleece, three body shapes from the purple fleece, and eighteen spots from the cream fleece.

3. Use the flower template on page 128 to trace and cut out three flowers from the pink fleece and three circular flower centers from the yellow fleece.

4. Baste the butterfly wings and then the body shapes onto the center of the pink fleece squares, then baste six spots (three on each side) onto the three sets of wings.

5. Blanket-stitch first around the body using two strands of the yellow floss, and then around the wings using two strands of the pink floss, and, finally, around the spots using two strands of the purple floss. Trace the butterfly antennas, then backstitch them using two strands of the purple floss. Stitch two purple French knots for the eyes and larger pink French knots for the noses.

6. Baste the three 7-inch cream fleece squares onto the center of the three 12-inch purple fleece squares. Then baste the pink fleece flowers and their circular yellow centers onto each of the cream squares.

7. Blanket-stitch around the cream squares using two strands of the yellow floss, around the flowers using two strands of the purple floss, and around the circular flower centers using two strands of the pink floss.

8. To assemble the blanket, refer to the Piecing a Quilt or Blanket section on page 12. Sew the first row so that a butterfly square is on the left and a flower square is on the right. Alternate the second row so that a flower square is on the left and a butterfly square is on the right. Sew the final row in the same manner as the first, with

the butterfly square on the left and the flower square on the right.

9. With the center seams aligned, sew the first and second rows together, then sew the final row to complete the top of the blanket.

10. Measure the length and width of the blanket, then cut a piece of cream fleece that's the same size to serve as the backing.

11. With the edges aligned, pin the two blanket pieces right sides together. Sew around the edges, leaving an opening wide enough at the bottom for turning. Trim the corners, then turn the piece right side out and slip stitch the opening closed.

Lullaby Lambs (Baby Sleeping) Door Hanger

It's easier than you think to create this project using scraps of wool felt and store-bought sheep iron-on appliqués. The embroidered details add vintage charm, while reminding visitors that Baby's naptime is in progress. As a fun variation, you can use the stitching to personalize the pillow with the little sleeper's name or date of birth.

WHAT YOU NEED

Basic materials, tools, and equipment (page 17)

Grass hill, clouds, and circular flower templates (page 129)

Scraps of pale green, blue, pink, and yellow wool felt

2 pieces of cream wool felt, each 8½ x 6½ inches

Ecru cotton embroidery floss

3 pearl beads, 4 mm diameter

3 iron-on sheep appliqués, each 2 inches wide

Polyester fiberfill

12 inches of ivory ribbon, ¼ inch wide

2 pieces of ivory ribbon, each ⅛ x 9 inches

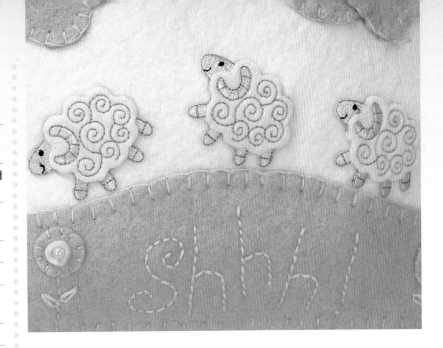

WHAT YOU DO

1. Use the templates on page 129 to trace and cut out one grass hill from the pale green felt, three clouds from the blue felt, three circular flowers from the pink felt, and three circular flower centers from the yellow felt.

2. Baste the grass hill onto the bottom of one of the cream felt pieces, then blanket-stitch along the top of the hill using three strands of the ecru floss.

3. Refer to the template or photo for placement, then baste the three clouds near the top, one at

the far left and two overlapping on the right. Blanket-stitch around the clouds using three strands of the ecru floss.

4. Baste the three pink flower circles and the yellow flower centers, two at the far left and the other at the far right. Once again, refer to the template or project photo for placement. Straight stitch (or blanket-stitch) around the pink flowers with the ecru floss, then stitch a pearl bead onto the center of the yellow circles. Using three strands of the ecru floss, backstitch the flower stems and use a Lazy Daisy stitch for the leaves.

5. Trace the "Shhh!" onto the grass hill, then backstitch it, using three strands of the ecru floss.

6. Iron the three sheep appliqués along the top of the grass hill. To make the appliqués extra secure, add a few stitches using matching or invisible thread.

7. With the edges aligned, place the two cream felt pieces wrong sides together. Blanket-stitch around the edges using three strands of the ecru floss, leaving an opening wide enough for stuffing.

8. Stuff the pillow with polyester fiberfill, then blanket-stitch the opening closed.

9. Stitch the ends of the ¼-inch ivory ribbon piece onto the top sides of the pillow for a hanger.

10. Tie two bows with the ⅛-inch ivory ribbon, then stitch the bows onto the ends of the ribbon hanger.

Every mom wants her little one to be dressed in style. With our Cutie Pie projects, you can make a fashion statement while pampering your tot in cozy comfort. Using our quick and easy embellishing techniques, you'll learn how to transform ordinary store-bought T-shirts, booties, and other wearables into extraordinary designer duds. With chic baby bibs, and darling scarf, mitten, and purse ensembles, your pint-size fashionista will be on the best-dressed list for years to come.

Cute as a Button Critter Cap

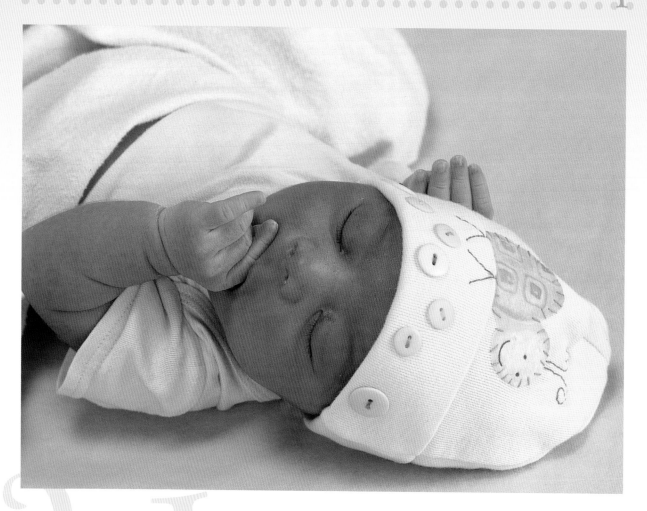

Using a simple fusible web technique, it's easy to embellish a plain baby cap. Decorative embroidery stitches and button trims add the perfect finishing touch. You can use this same technique as inspiration to dress up other store-bought clothing items, such as pants and T-shirts.

WHAT YOU DO

1. Apply the fusible web onto the print fabric (see Fusible Web Appliqué, page 12), then cut out the bug or critter motif. Fuse the motif onto the front center of the baby cap.

2. Straight stitch around the motif, using two strands of matching floss.

3. Using two strands of matching floss, backstitch decorative details such as legs and antennas.

4. Stitch the seven buttons along the bottom of the cap.

WHAT YOU NEED

Basic materials, tools, and equipment (page 17)

Fusible web

Piece of print fabric with a bug or critter motif, 3 x 2 inches

Prewashed knit baby cap

Cotton embroidery floss to match critter motif

7 assorted buttons

Shabby "Chick" T-Shirt, Hanger, Booties, and Socks

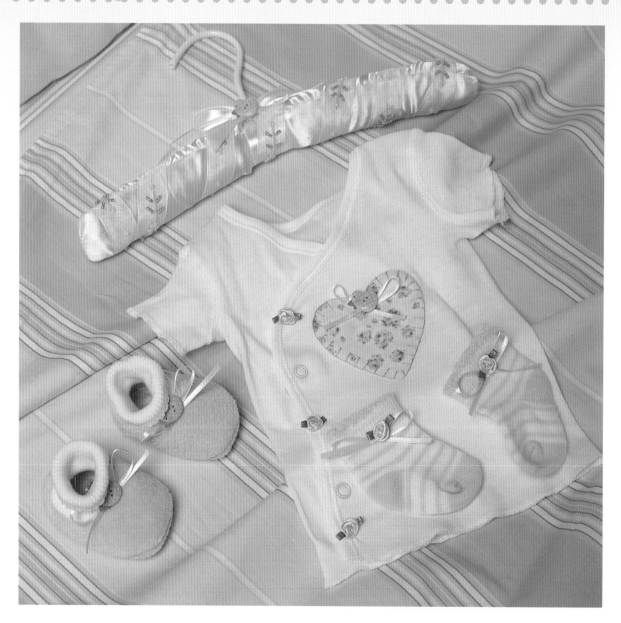

With some scraps of fabric and a few crafty trims, you can transform a plain-Jane T-shirt, hanger, and other wearables into a fashionable clothing ensemble. A heart-shaped appliqué adds a touch of vintage chic to the cotton shirt, which is further embellished with a charming chick button and romantic rosebud trims. Coordinate the look by stitching similar trims onto matching socks and booties.

To make the T-shirt:

WHAT YOU NEED

Basic materials, tools, and equipment (page 17)

Heart template (page 131) (Use the one that's on the bunny)

Fusible web

Scrap of pink floral print fabric

Prewashed white cotton snap-on T-shirt (I used a 3- to 6-month size.)

Pink cotton embroidery floss

9 inches of pink ribbon, ⅛ inch wide

Pink chick button

3 pink ribbon rosebuds with flat green bows

Note: To protect Baby's skin from the embroidered stitching on the heart appliqué, add a square- or heart-shaped lining to the inside of the T-shirt using a heavyweight (no-sew) brand of fusible web and a small scrap of white cotton fabric or flannel. Another option is to sew around the heart appliqué using a zigzag or satin stitch.

WHAT YOU DO

1. Apply the fusible web onto the floral print fabric (see Fusible Web Appliqué, page 12), then trace and cut out the heart template on page 131. Fuse the heart shape onto the front of the T-shirt, then blanket-stitch around the heart shape using two strands of the pink floss.

2. Tie a bow with the ⅛-inch pink ribbon and stitch it onto the top center of the heart. Then stitch the pink chick button onto the center of the bow.

3. Stitch the three pink ribbon rosebuds in between the snaps of the T-shirt, spacing the rosebuds evenly.

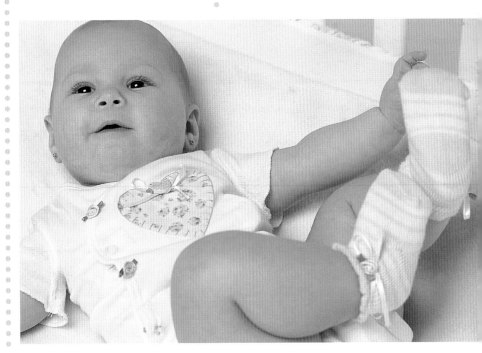

To make the hanger:

WHAT YOU NEED

Basic materials, tools, and equipment (page 17)

White satin padded hanger with bow

34 inches of beaded pink flowered ribbon, ⅞ inch wide

15 inches of pink ribbon, ⅛ inch wide

Pink chick button

WHAT YOU DO

1. Stitch one end of the beaded pink ribbon onto the back of the far left side of the hanger, then wrap the ribbon around the hanger until you reach the far right side, making sure the ribbon is spaced evenly. Then stitch the other end of the ribbon onto the back of the hanger until it's secure. Add extra stitches as necessary to secure the ribbon.

2. Tie a bow with the ⅛-inch pink ribbon and stitch it to the white satin bow on the center of the hanger. Then stitch the pink chick button onto the center of the two bows.

To make the booties:

WHAT YOU NEED

Basic materials, tools, and equipment (page 17)

Pair of prewashed pink and white baby booties

2 pieces of pink ribbon, each ⅛ x 9 inches

2 pink chick buttons

WHAT YOU DO

1. Tie two bows with the ⅛-inch pink ribbon, then stitch the bows onto the booties in the center of each cuff.

2. Stitch the pink chick buttons onto the center of the bows.

To make the socks:

WHAT YOU NEED

Basic materials, tools, and equipment (page 17)

Pair of prewashed pink and white baby socks

2 pieces of pink ribbon, each ⅛ x 9 inches

2 pink ribbon rosebuds with flat green bows, each 1 inch wide

WHAT YOU DO

1. Tie two bows with the ⅛-inch pink ribbon, then stitch the bows onto the outer top side of each sock.

2. Stitch the pink ribbon rosebuds onto the center of the bows.

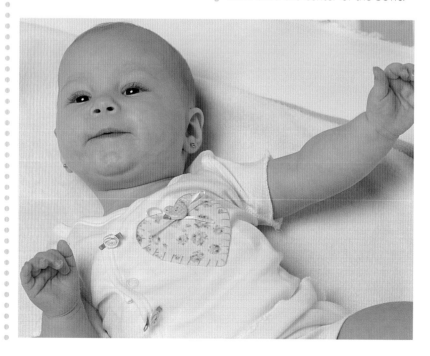

Designer Denim Bibs

What a unique *way* to recycle an old pair of jeans. Everyone knows how tough denim is—these sturdy-but-fun bibs will stand up to whatever your tot dishes out.

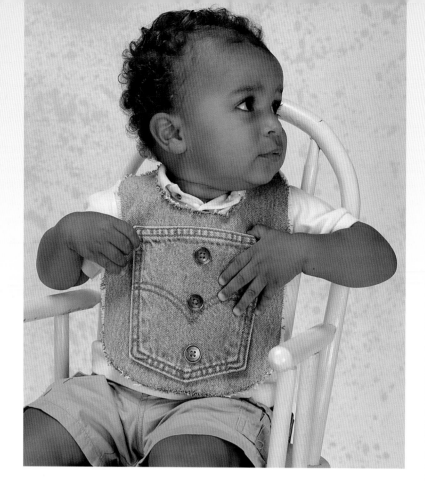

outer edges of the bib, being careful not to rip the stitched seam.

5. Cut out a pocket from the pair of jeans, then stitch the three metal buttons along the center of the pocket.

6. Pin the pocket to the center of the bib, then secure the pocket around the inner side and bottom edges using a running stitch and three strands of the matching floss. Leave the top side of the pocket open.

7. Adhere the round hook-and-loop fastener onto each side of the neck closure.

To make the pocket bib:

WHAT YOU NEED

Basic materials, tools, and equipment (page 17)

Bib template (page 128)

Pair of old jeans

Seam ripper

Round hook-and-loop fastener, ⅝-inch diameter

Jean pocket, 6½ inches

3 metal buttons

Cotton embroidery floss to match stitching on jeans (I use orange.)

WHAT YOU DO

1. Cut apart the legs of the jeans for a piece of denim fabric large enough to fit the bib template, then iron the fabric to remove any creases and wrinkles.

2. Trace and cut out the bib shape on page 128 from the denim fabric (ignore the dotted lines on the template).

3. Sew along the edges of the bib, using a ¼-inch seam allowance.

4. With the seam ripper, fray the

To make the purse bib:

WHAT YOU NEED

Basic materials, tools, and
equipment (page 17)

Bib template (page 128)

Pair of old jeans

Seam ripper

Round hook-and-loop fastener,
⅜-inch diameter

3 iron-on flower appliqués

WHAT YOU DO

1. Cut apart the legs of the jeans
for a piece of denim fabric large
enough to fit the bib template, then
iron the fabric.

2. Trace and cut out the bib
shape on page 128 from the denim
fabric. Then trace and cut out the
top section of the bib that will be
the flap of the purse, indicated by
the template's dotted lines.

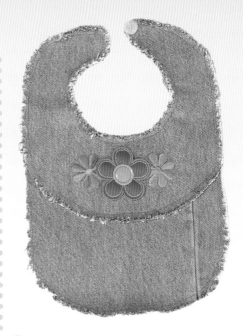

3. Sew along the edges of the
main bib shape, using a ¼-inch seam
allowance. It's only necessary to
sew along the bottom half, which is
the area that remains visible after
the top section is added.

4. With the edges aligned, baste
the top section onto the bib, then
sew along the remaining edges and
the inner flap using a ¼-inch seam
allowance.

5. With the seam ripper, fray the
outer edges of the bib, being careful
not to rip the stitched seam.

6. Iron on the three flower
appliqués, adding a few stitches
using matching or invisible thread to
secure them.

7. Adhere the hook-and-loop
fastener onto each side of the
neck closure.

Busy Bee Slippers

These delightful bee slippers will create quite a buzz while keeping your tot's tootsies warm and cozy. They're easy to make using a pair of yellow fleece slippers, scraps of felt, and simple embroidery stitches. Sweet as honey and cute as can "bee," these slippers would also make an adorable baby shower gift.

WHAT YOU NEED

Basic materials, tools, and equipment (page 17)

Bee head template (page 127)

Felt or wool felt scraps in black and cream

Cotton embroidery floss in yellow and black

Polyester fiberfill

Four black pom-poms, each 7 mm

Pair of yellow prewashed fleece baby booties or slippers

WHAT YOU DO

1. Use the bee head template on page 127 to trace and cut out four circular head shapes from the black felt and two inner face shapes from the cream felt.

2. Baste the two cream felt faces onto the center of two of the black felt circles.

3. Blanket-stitch around the faces using two strands of the yellow floss. Use the black floss to stitch two French knots for the eyes. Stitch larger French knots for the noses with the yellow floss.

4. Place the stitched bee heads wrong sides together with the remaining black felt circles. Blanket-stitch around the outer edges of each bee head using two strands of

the yellow floss, leaving an opening wide enough for stuffing.

5. Stuff each bee head with small pieces of polyester fiberfill, then blanket-stitch the opening closed.

6. Stitch two black pom-poms onto the top of each bee head.

7. Stitch a bee head onto the front flap of each slipper.

8. For the two black stripes, measure the width of the slipper where the stripes will be positioned. My top stripe is 4 inches and my bottom

stripe is 3¼ inches, based on a large slipper size. These measurements will vary depending on the size of the slipper used. (My stripes are ⅝ inch wide.)

9. Cut the two stripes out of the black felt, then baste them in the desired position. Blanket-stitch around the stripes, using two strands of the yellow floss. Repeat for the other slipper.

Fleecy Friends Bibs

For those special holiday meals and celebrations, dress Baby up in one of our soft and sweet critter bibs. These furry friends also make darling accents to brighten up your nursery décor. Older tots can use the bibs to dress up teddy bears and other tea party guests.

To make the lamb bib:

WHAT YOU NEED

Basic materials, tools, and equipment (page 17)

Lamb bib template (page 129)

⅓ yard sherpa polar fleece

Scraps of tan plush felt

Dark brown cotton embroidery floss

Pink button

Polyester fiberfill

Round hook-and-loop fastener, ⅝ inch diameter

WHAT YOU DO

1. Using the lamb bib template on page 129, trace and cut out two bib shapes from the cream polar fleece.

2. Use the template on page 129 to trace and cut out one face and two ear shapes from the tan plush felt.

3. Trace the mouth onto the right side of the face, then back-stitch the mouth using six strands of the brown floss. Stitch the pink button at the top of the mouth.

4. With the brown floss, make two French knots for the eyes.

5. Baste the face and the two ear shapes onto the right side of one of the bib pieces. Blanket-stitch around the face and ears, using six strands of the brown floss.

6. With the edges aligned, pin the two bib pieces wrong sides together. Blanket-stitch around the bib shape, using six strands of the brown floss and leaving an opening wide enough for stuffing. Stuff the face area of the bib with polyester fiberfill to give it some dimension, then blanket-stitch the opening closed.

7. Adhere the hook-and-loop fastener onto each side of the neck closure.

To make the puppy bib:

WHAT YOU NEED

Basic materials, tools, and equipment (page 17)

Puppy bib template (page 129)

⅓ yard tan plush felt

Felt scraps in dark brown, cream, and dark gray or black

Cotton embroidery floss in dark brown and ecru

Polyester fiberfill

Round hook-and-loop fastener, ⅝ inch diameter

WHAT YOU DO

1. Using the puppy bib template on page 129, trace and cut out two bib shapes and two puppy ear shapes from the tan plush felt.

2. Use the template on page 129 to trace and cut out five spots from the dark brown felt, one nose from the dark gray or black felt, and two small circular eyes from the cream felt.

3. Trace the mouth onto the right side of one of the bib pieces, then backstitch the mouth with six strands of the brown floss.

4. Baste the nose at the top of the mouth, then blanket-stitch around the nose, using three strands of the ecru floss. Using the nose as a center guide, baste the two eyes. Then backstitch an inner circle around each eye using three strands of the brown floss, and satin stitch the two pupils.

5. Baste the five spots onto the front of the ears, then baste the two ear shapes onto the bib. Blanket-stitch around the spots and the outer edges of the ears using three strands of the ecru floss.

6. With the edges aligned, pin the two bib pieces wrong sides together. Then blanket-stitch around the bib shape with six strands of the brown floss, leaving an opening wide enough for stuffing. Stuff the face area of the bib with polyester fiberfill to give it some dimension, and blanket-stitch the opening closed.

7. Adhere the hook-and-loop fastener onto each side of the neck closure.

See Ya Later Alligator

Scarf and Mittens

Look *what we found* lurking in *the swamp.* This bold and bright alligator scarf and mitten set is perfect for keeping *tots toasty* warm in the cold winter months. To adjust for size variations, simply photocopy the templates to enlarge or reduce them as desired.

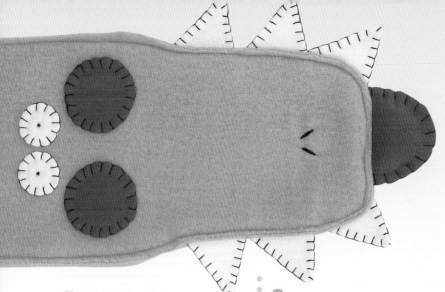

To make the scarf:

WHAT YOU NEED

Basic materials, tools, and equipment (page 17)

Alligator scarf template (page 130)

2 pieces of lime green fleece, each 5½ x 44 inches

Felt or wool felt scraps in red and cream or white

Black cotton embroidery floss

Polyester fiberfill

WHAT YOU DO

1. Use the template on page 130 to trace the shape of the alligator head onto one end of each of the fleece scarf pieces (see figure 1). Then cut along the traced lines of the head.

Place template at one end of each piece of fleece.

Cut around template.

Figure 1

2. Use the same template to trace two eyes and 12 teeth onto the white or cream felt, and two cheeks and two tongues onto the red felt. Then cut out each piece.

3. Baste the two eyes and two cheeks onto one of the scarf pieces, using the photo or template for placement. Then blanket-stitch around each piece with two strands of the black floss. Stitch a French knot with the black floss in the center of each eye.

4. Use two strands of the black floss to satin stitch the two nostrils.

5. With the edges aligned, pin the two tongue shapes together. Using two strands of the black floss, blanket-stitch around the tongue, leaving the top straight edge open. Then stuff the tongue sparingly with small pieces of polyester fiberfill.

6. With the edges aligned, baste the 12 tooth shapes to form a total of six teeth. Using two strands of the black floss, blanket-stitch around the tooth shapes. You can leave the straight top edge of each tooth open, as it will be concealed when the teeth are sewn into the scarf.

7. With the edges aligned, place the two scarf pieces wrong sides together, then baste the two pieces with the tongue and teeth sandwiched in between. The tongue should be in the center with three teeth on each side. If desired, add pins for extra security. Finally, sew along the edges of the scarf, using a ¼-inch seam allowance.

To make the mittens:

WHAT YOU NEED

Basic materials, tools, and equipment (page 17)

Alligator mitten template (page 130)

4 pieces of lime green fleece, each 6 x 8 ½ inches

Felt or wool felt scraps in red and cream or white

2 pieces of elastic, each ⅜ x 6 inches (See Note below)

Black cotton embroidery floss

Note: I find it easier to sew the elastic if the pieces are cut somewhat longer than needed—in this case, approximately 7 inches, with the excess elastic trimmed after it's sewn.

Note: **Although these mittens were designed for older tots approximately three to four years old, to be safe, simply trace your tot's hand onto paper and use the pattern as a guide. Then enlarge or reduce the pattern as necessary. Remember, little gators grow quickly, so it's best to overestimate the size requirements for your mittens rather than making them too small.**

WHAT YOU DO

1. Use the alligator mitten template on page 130 to trace and cut out four mitten shapes from the lime green fleece, and 12 claw shapes from the cream or white felt.

2. With the edges aligned, pin both pairs of mittens right sides together. Sew the mittens approximately 4 inches down from the top straight edge of the wrist, using a ¼-inch seam allowance (see figure 2). When you open up each mitten, the two pieces will now be joined in the center (see figure 3).

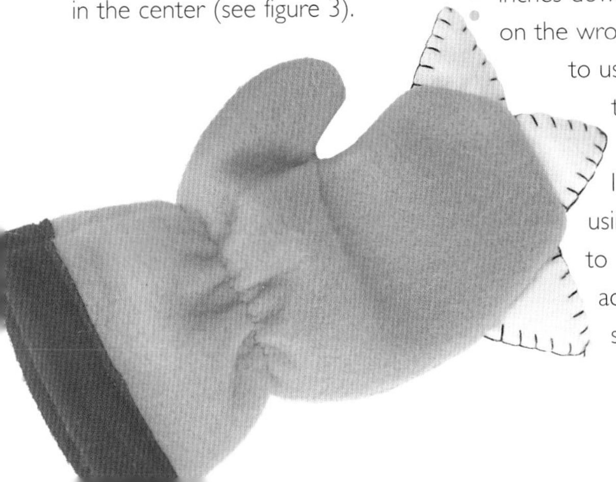

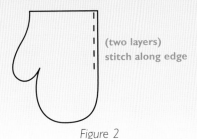

(two layers)
stitch along edge

Figure 2

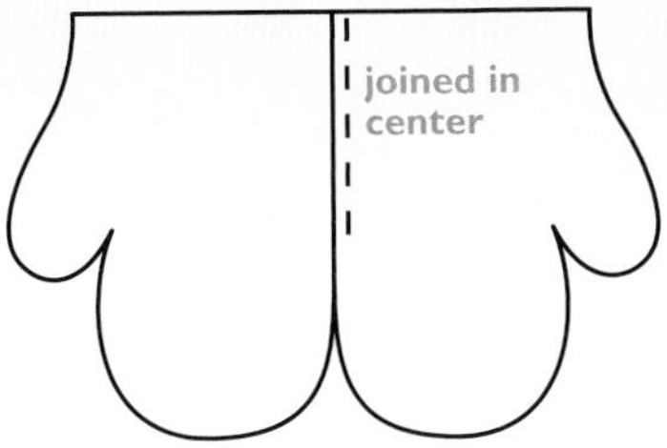

joined in
center

Figure 3

3. Open up one of the mittens and measure the width along the top straight edge of the wrist. Using this measurement, cut a 2-inch-wide strip from the red felt to use as a border. Do the same for the other mitten.

4. For each mitten, fold the red felt strip in half lengthwise, then pin the strip over the top straight edge, and sew it in place.

5. Draw a line approximately 3 inches down from the straight edge on the wrong side of each mitten to use as a guide for stitching the elastic. Place the elastic strip along the guideline and sew it in place, using a zigzag stitch. Be sure to stretch the elastic to fit across the width as you're sewing. Trim any excess elastic.

6. With the edges aligned, baste the 12 claw shapes together to form a total of six claws. Blanket-stitch around the claw shapes, using two strands of black floss. You can leave the straight bottom edge of each claw open, as it will be concealed when the claw is sewn onto the mitten.

7. Open up one of the mittens right side facing upwards. Position three of the claws onto one of the mitten pieces so they are pointing upwards to the wrist, with the straight bottom edge of the claws facing the curved outer edge of the mitten (see figure 4).

8. Pin the two mitten layers right sides together with the claws sandwiched in between. Using a ¼-inch seam allowance, sew the layers together along the outer edge of the mitten from the 4-inch stitch line (sewn in step 2) to the cuff. Trim the corners by the thumb, then turn the mitten right side out. Repeat these steps for the other mitten.

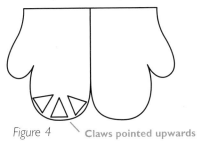

Right sides facing up

Figure 4 ＼ **Claws pointed upwards**

SEWING FOR TINY TOTS

Chic Kitty Purse and Scarf

Ooh la la! This chic, kitty-inspired ensemble is "purr-fect" for the mini fashion diva. Created from animal print fleece and scraps of felt, the stylish purse and scarf are sure to turn heads. The fluffy pink marabou and pom-pom trims add a fabulously feminine touch to complete the designer look.

To make the purse:

WHAT YOU NEED

Basic materials, tools and equipment (page 17)

Cat template (page 130)

Felt or wool felt scraps in tan, pink and cream

Piece of leopard print fleece, 10 x 20 inches

Black cotton embroidery floss

15 inches of pink-and-white checkered ribbon, ⅞ inch wide

Pink ribbon rosebud with green leaves, 1¼ inches wide

22 inches of pink pom-pom trim, 1 inch wide

14 inches of pink marabou, 1½ inches wide

3 inches of hook-and-loop tape, ¾ inch wide

WHAT YOU DO

1. Use the cat template on page 130 to trace and cut out one cat head from the tan felt, one muzzle shape from the cream felt, and the nose and two inner ear pieces from the pink felt.

2. Fold the 10 x 20-inch piece of leopard fleece in half so you have a piece that's 10 inches square. Make sure that the folded edge of the fleece square is facing the bottom. Referring to the photo or template for placement, baste the felt cat

pieces onto the fleece square in the center, approximately 1 to 1½ inches from the bottom fold.

3. Lay the piece of leopard fleece flat, right side facing upwards. Blanket-stitch around the cat head, muzzle, nose, and inner ears using two strands of the black floss.

4. Beginning at the center of the nose, trace and then backstitch a line onto the muzzle using two strands of the black floss. Add a black French knot at the bottom of the line for the mouth.

5. Trace and then backstitch three whiskers onto each side of the face using two strands of the black floss.

6. With the black floss, add two French knots just above the nose for the eyes.

7. Tie a bow with the pink-and-white ribbon. Stitch the bow and the pink rosebud trim onto the bottom of the cat.

8. Fold and pin the piece of fleece in half, right sides together. Using a ¼-inch seam allowance, sew along the two side edges. Leave the top edge open.

9. Turn the fleece right side out, then stitch the pink pom-pom trim around the top edge of the purse. Stitch the piece of pink marabou onto the top inner sides of the purse for a handle.

10. Adhere the hook-and-loop tape onto the top inside edges of the purse.

To make the scarf:

WHAT YOU NEED

Basic materials, tools and equipment (page 17)

Scraps of tan felt or wool felt

2 pieces of leopard print fleece, each 6 x 44 inches

Black cotton embroidery floss

Paw print template (page 130)

2 pieces of pink marabou, each 1½ x 5½ inches

WHAT YOU DO

1. Trace and cut out two paw print templates on page 130 from the tan felt.

2. Baste the paw prints onto one of the leopard print fleece pieces, approximately 2½ inches from the edge of each side (see figure 1). Position the paws so the toes are facing the center of the scarf. Blanket-stitch around the two paw prints using two strands of the black floss.

3. With the edges aligned, pin the two scarf pieces right sides together. Sew along the edges of the scarf using a ¼-inch seam allowance, leaving an opening large enough at one end for turning. Turn right side out, then slip stitch the opening closed.

4. Stitch a piece of pink marabou onto each end of the scarf.

↑ 2½"

facing center

↑ 2½"

Figure 1

Figure 1

CHAPTER THREE

Gifts & Giggles

FUN AND UNIQUE GIFT IDEAS

Our one-of-a-kind collection of gift ideas is guaranteed to make kids of all ages giggle with delight. A cupcake decorating party is a great way to start the fun, with rainbow-bright blankets, aprons, and favor bags that look good enough to eat. Our super soft giraffe blanket and chenille bunny are sure to keep them smiling. There's even a cheery cow bag that can make laundry day a time for play. With so many fresh and creative ideas, you'll have them giggling in no time!

Chenille Snuggle Bunny and Mini Quilt

Sugar and spice and everything nice—that's what this bunny is made of. Treat your little princess to this oh-so-sweet chenille bunny, a perfect playmate for those imaginary tea parties and stuffed animal sleepovers. Exuding old-fashioned charm with her vintage heart motif and dainty rosebud trims, this cuddly companion and her snuggly quilt are the perfect gift idea.

To make the bunny:

WHAT YOU NEED

Basic materials, tools, and equipment (page 17)

Bunny template (page 131)

⅓ yard of cream chenille fabric

Fusible web

Scraps of pink floral print fabric

Cotton embroidery floss in pink and dark brown

Pink ribbon flower accent with green bows, 1¼ inches

2 pieces of pink ribbon, each ⅛ x 9 inches

2 pink ribbon rosebuds with flat green bows, each 1 inch

6¾ inches of pink and green lace flower trim, ⅜ inch wide

3 pink ribbon rosebuds with green leaves, each 1¼ inch

Polyester fiberfill

WHAT YOU DO

1. Use the bunny template on page 131 to trace and cut out two bunny shapes from the cream chenille fabric.

2. Apply the fusible web onto the floral print fabric (see Fusible Web Appliqué, page 12), then trace and cut out the heart shape and the two inner ear shapes on page 131. Referring to the photo or template for placement, fuse the inner ear and heart shapes onto the front of one of the chenille bunny pieces.

3. Blanket-stitch around the inner ear and heart shapes, using two strands of the pink floss.

4. Cut the green bows off the 1¼-inch pink ribbon flower accent, then stitch the flower accent onto the center of the bunny's face for the nose. Backstitch a 1½-inch line straight down from the center of the nose using six strands of the brown floss. Then stitch two brown French knots for the eyes.

5. Tie two bows with the pink ribbon, then stitch the bows onto the top center of the heart and the bottom center of the left inner ear. Stitch the 1-inch pink ribbon rosebuds onto the center of the bows.

6. Sew the lace flower trim onto the neck of the bunny, then stitch the three 1¼-inch pink ribbon rosebuds along the neck trim, spacing them out evenly.

7. With the edges aligned, pin the two chenille bunny pieces right sides together. Sew the bunny pieces together using a ¼-inch seam allowance and leaving an opening at the bottom wide enough for stuffing.

8. Trim the corners, then turn the bunny right side out, stuff it with polyester fiberfill, and slip stitch the opening closed.

To make the quilt:

WHAT YOU NEED

Heart template from bunny
(page 131), or heart cookie cutter,
3 inches

Scrap of pink floral print fabric

Fusible web

3 pieces of cream chenille
fabric, one 5 inches square,
two 16 inches square

Cotton embroidery floss in pink
and ecru

9 inches of pink ribbon,
⅛ inch wide

5 pink ribbon rosebuds with flat
green bows, each 1 inch

2 pieces of pink chenille fabric,
each 10 inches square

2 pieces of quilt batting,
one 9 inches square,
one 15 inches square

tip To save time, make the quilt in the traditional manner by
piecing the entire top together first, without stuffing and
sewing the center block separately. You would then need only
one piece of the pink chenille fabric and only the 15-inch piece
of quilt batting. Another option is to use the pink center block
itself as a tinier version of the quilt, without piecing it onto the
larger background square of cream chenille.

WHAT YOU DO

*To make the mini pink quilt
for the center block:*

1. Refer to step 2 on the previous page to make the floral heart
appliqué, then fuse the heart shape
onto the right side of the 5-inch
cream chenille square in the center.

2. Blanket-stitch around the
heart shape, using two strands of
the pink floss.

3. Tie a bow with the pink
ribbon, and stitch it onto the top
center of the heart. Then stitch a
pink ribbon rosebud onto the
center of the bow.

4. Baste the cream chenille heart
square onto the right side of one of
the pink chenille squares in the center, then blanket-stitch around the
edges of the cream square using
two strands of the pink floss.

5. Baste the 9-inch piece of
batting in between the top and
bottom layers of the quilt. Make
sure the batting is positioned in the
center, with the wrong sides of the
pink chenille quilt top and backing
facing together.

6. Pin the three layers together,
sew around the edges of the quilt
using a ⅜- to ½-inch seam
allowance, then stitch along each
side of the center square, all the
way to the outer edges.

7. Stitch each of the other four pink ribbon rosebuds onto the corners of the cream chenille heart square.

To cut and piece the rest of the quilt:

8. Baste the mini pink quilt block onto the center of one of the 16-inch cream chenille squares, then sew a running stitch along the edges of the pink center block to secure it, using six strands of the ecru floss.

9. Baste the 15-inch piece of batting in between the top and bottom layers of the quilt, making sure it's positioned in the center, with the wrong sides of the cream chenille quilt top and backing facing together.

10. Pin the three layers together, sew around the edges of the quilt using a ⅜- to ½-inch seam allowance, then stitch along each side of the center square, all the way to the outer edges.

11. Using six strands of the pink floss, sew a running stitch around the four corners and outer edges of the cream chenille background.

Cupcake Cutie Blanket, Apron, and Favor Bags

Kids love cupcakes. With that in mind, we've cooked up this yummy collection of sweet treats, perfect for a cupcake decorating party theme. Spruce up the cake table with a colorful confetti cupcake blanket, while presenting the guest of honor with her very own pint-size chef apron. Our darling cupcake favor bags look good enough to eat. Filled with delicious discoveries such as miniature cooking utensils, candy sprinkles, cookie cutters, fun-filled recipes, and other baking delights, they're sure to enchant aspiring chefs of all ages.

To make the blanket:

WHAT YOU NEED

Basic materials, tools, and equipment (page 17)

Cupcake template (page 130)

Felt or wool felt scraps in pink, dark brown, and cream

9 pieces of pink, white, and green candy stripe ribbon, each ⅝ x 5 inches

Iron-on adhesive hem or fusible web tape, ⅝ inch wide

Cotton embroidery floss in dark brown and pink

2 pieces of pink multicolor dot fleece, each 29 x 35 inches

40 inches of jumbo pink chenille rickrack

3 pieces of pink polka-dot ribbon, each ⅜ x 13 inches

3 mini pink flower iron-on appliqués, each ¾ inch wide

9 pink ribbon flower accents with green bows, each 1¼ inches wide

3 iridescent pink pom-poms, each ½ inch

WHAT YOU DO

1. Use the cupcake template on page 130 to trace and cut out three cupcake bottoms from the pink felt, three cupcake tops from the dark brown felt, and three icing trim shapes from the cream felt.

2. Cut nine 5-inch pieces of the candy stripe ribbon and the adhesive hem or fusible tape. Following the manufacturer's instructions, apply the adhesive hem or fusible tape onto the ribbon pieces. Beginning with the center stripe, adhere three of the ribbon pieces, spaced evenly, onto the three cupcake bottoms. For extra security, add a few stitches at the ends using matching or invisible thread.

3. Referring to the photo and template for placement, baste the

tip

To save time, you may prefer to sew the edges of the blanket instead of using the blanket-stitch embroidery technique. If you machine stitch, remember to pin the two blanket pieces right sides together, leaving an opening large enough at the bottom for turning. After turning, simply slip stitch the opening closed.

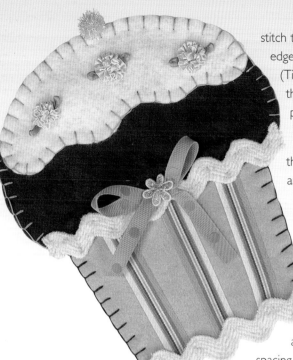

stitch them along the bottom edges of the cupcakes. (Tip: Use fray retardant on the ends of the rickrack to prevent fraying.)

6. Tie three bows with the pink polka-dot ribbon, and stitch them onto the center of the top rickrack trim. Then adhere the pink flower appliqués to the centers of the bows.

7. Stitch three of the pink ribbon flower accents along the icing trim, spacing them out evenly as you work. Then stitch a pink pom-pom onto the top center of the icing trim for a cherry. Repeat for the remaining cupcakes.

8. With the edges aligned, pin the two blanket pieces wrong sides together. Then blanket-stitch around the edges, using six strands of the brown floss.

To decorate the apron:

WHAT YOU NEED

Basic materials, tools, and equipment (page 17)

Child's chef apron with bottom pocket divider

three cupcakes onto one of the fleece blanket pieces.

4. Blanket-stitch around the top of the cupcakes and the icing trim with three strands of the pink floss, and around the bottom of the cupcakes (sides only) with three strands of the brown floss. (Tip: There is no need to embroider the two edges where the rickrack will be adhered, since the stitches will be covered anyway.)

5. Cut three 8-inch pieces of the pink rickrack trim. Baste, then stitch the three pieces along the top edges of the cupcakes. Then cut three 5¼-inch pieces of the pink rickrack trim. Baste the pieces, then

To make the cupcake appliqué:

Cupcake template (page 130)

Felt or wool felt scraps in pink, dark brown, and cream

3 pieces of pink, white, and green candy stripe ribbon, each ⅝ x 4½ inches

Iron-on adhesive hem or fusible web tape, ⅝ inch wide

Cotton embroidery floss in dark brown and pink

2 pieces of jumbo pink chenille rickrack, one 6½ inches long, one 4¾ inches long

13 inches of pink polka-dot ribbon, ⅜ inch wide

Mini pink flower iron-on appliqué, ¾ inch wide

3 pink ribbon flower accents with green bows, each 1¼ inches wide

Iridescent pink pom-pom, ½ inch

To embellish the pocket:

Iron-on adhesive hem or fusible web tape, ⅞ inch wide and ⅝ inch wide

Brown and pink polka-dot ribbon, 1½ x 16½ inches, or to fit width of apron

Brown and pink striped ribbon, ⅞ x 16½ inches, or to fit width of apron

Jumbo pink chenille rickrack, 16½ inches, or to fit width of apron

5 pink ribbon flower accents with green bows, each 1¼ inches wide

WHAT YOU DO

1. Use the cupcake template on page 130 to trace and cut out a cupcake bottom from the pink felt, a cupcake top from the dark brown felt, and an icing trim shape from the cream felt.

2. Cut three 4½-inch pieces of the candy stripe ribbon and the ⅝-inch adhesive hem or fusible tape. Following the manufacturer's instructions, apply the adhesive hem or fusible tape onto the ribbon pieces. Beginning with the center stripe, adhere the three ribbon pieces, spaced evenly, onto the cupcake bottom. For extra security, add a few stitches at the ends using matching or invisible thread.

3. Using the photo and template for placement, baste the cupcake onto the front center of the apron.

4. Blanket-stitch around the top of the cupcake and the icing trim with three strands of the pink floss, and around the bottom of the cupcake (sides only) with three strands of the brown floss. (Tip: There is no need to embroider the two edges where the rickrack will be adhered, since the stitches will be covered anyway.)

5. Baste, then stitch the 6½-inch piece of rickrack along the top edge of the cupcake and the 4¾-inch piece along the bottom edge of the cupcake. (Tip: Use fray retardant on

the ends of the rickrack to prevent fraying.)

6. Tie a bow with the pink polka-dot ribbon, and stitch it to the center of the top row of rickrack trim. Then adhere the pink flower appliqué to the center of the bow.

7. Stitch the three pink ribbon flower accents along the icing trim, spacing the accents out evenly as you work. Then stitch a pink pom-pom onto the top center of the icing trim for a cherry.

8. Using strips of the ⅞ inch and the ⅝ inch adhesive hem or fusible tape, adhere the brown and pink polka-dot ribbon approximately ½ inch from the top of the bottom pocket divider. For extra security, add a few stitches with matching or invisible thread. Using the same technique, use the ⅞ inch adhesive tape to adhere the brown and pink striped ribbon just below.

9. Baste, then stitch the piece of rickrack trim along the bottom edge of the apron.

10. Stitch the five pink ribbon flower accents, spacing three of them evenly along the center of the ribbon pieces, and one at each end.

WHAT YOU NEED

Basic materials, tools, and equipment (page 17)

1 piece of pink multicolor dot flannel or print fabric, 6 x 20 inches

2 pieces of iron-on adhesive hem, ⅜ x 6 inches (optional)

Cupcake template (page 130)

Felt or wool felt scraps in brown, cream, and the pastel color of your choice (pink, blue, yellow or green)

Cotton embroidery floss in dark brown and ecru

9 inches of ivory ribbon, ⅛ inch wide

Iridescent pom-pom in the pastel color of your choice (pink, blue, yellow, or green), ½ inch

Hot glue and hot-glue gun (optional)

Treats to fill bag

Curling ribbon

Personalized name tag (optional)

WHAT YOU DO

1. To make one bag, sew a ⅜-inch hem onto each end of the pink dot fabric, or use two 6-inch pieces of the iron-on adhesive hem. Following the manufacturer's instructions, iron the adhesive hem onto each end (wrong side) of the fabric. Then fold the ends over and iron them again to form a hem.

2. Fold the fabric piece in half wrong sides together, so that the folded edge is facing the bottom.

3. Referring to the cupcake template on page 130, trace and cut out the cupcake bottom from the pastel felt. Then trace and cut out the cupcake top from the brown felt and the icing trim shape from the cream felt.

4. Baste the cupcake pieces onto the folded piece of fabric, referring to the photo and template for placement. Once the felt pieces are basted in the desired position, lay the piece of fabric flat for stitching.

5. Blanket-stitch around the cupcake bottom and icing trim with two strands of the brown floss. Then blanket-stitch around the cupcake top with two strands of the ecru floss.

6. Tie a bow for the bag using the ivory ribbon, then stitch the bow and the pom-pom onto the cupcake. If you prefer, you can hot glue these pieces on at the very end.

7. With the edges aligned, pin the fabric piece in half, right sides together. Leaving the top side open, sew along the two sides of the bag using a ¼-inch seam allowance, then turn the bag right side out.

8. Fill the bag with treats and favors, or candy trims for decorating the cupcake. Tie the top of the bag closed with curling ribbon, and add a personalized name tag. If you're planning a party, make multiple bags and place one at each table setting—perfect for a sweet celebration!

Giraffe Cuddle Blanket

Brighten Baby's day with this colorful giraffe blanket. It's the perfect size for stroller rides or to roll up for take-along comfort. Your little one will love the vibrant colors and cozy softness of the boldly striped fleece. You'll love the simplicity of the design with its strip-tied edges and hand-stitched details.

WHAT YOU NEED

Basic materials, tools, and equipment (page 17)

Giraffe template (page 132)

Piece of yellow fleece or wool felt, 18 x 24 inches

Wool felt scraps in pastel blue, pink, and green

2 pieces of multicolor striped fleece, each 28 x 35 inches

Dark brown cotton embroidery floss

WHAT YOU DO

1. Use the giraffe template on page 132 to trace and cut out the giraffe shape from the yellow fleece (or felt), two hoofs and three spots from the blue felt, one nose, two inner ear pieces and three spots from the pink felt, and three mane pieces and two spots from the green felt.

2. Lay the giraffe piece lengthwise in the center of one of the multicolor fleece pieces. Using the photo or template for placement, position the three mane pieces so that the straight edges lie just underneath the neckline of the giraffe. Baste the giraffe and the three mane pieces, along with the two hoofs, the nose, the two inner ear pieces, and the eight spots. Blanket-stitch around all of the pieces using six strands of the brown floss.

3. With the edges aligned, pin the two blanket pieces wrong sides together.

4. Cut a 3-inch square from each corner (see figure 1). Then cut 3-inch-long fringes approximately 1 inch wide along each side of the blanket. Be sure to cut the fringes through both layers of the blanket.

5. Tie the fringes together to secure the two blanket pieces.

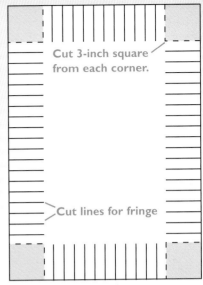

Cut 3-inch square from each corner.

Cut lines for fringe

Figure 1

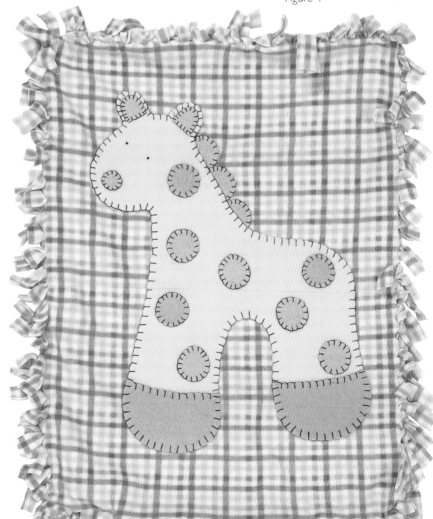

Bathtime Buddies Hooded Bath Towel

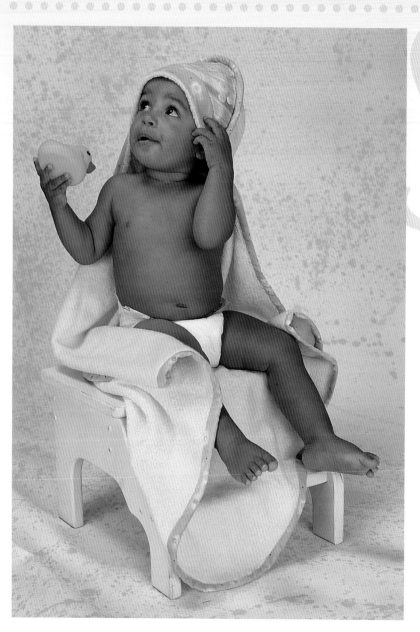

Splish splash—your tot will love taking a bath when snuggling up in this cheery hooded towel. Fashioned from plush terry cloth and pieced cotton prints, the hood is embellished with cute critter appliqués and colorful button trims. Perfect for on-the-go summer outings to the beach or pool.

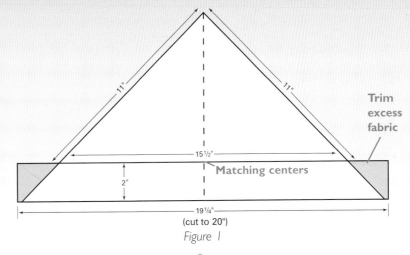

Figure 1

WHAT YOU NEED

Basic materials, tools, and equipment (page 17)

One yard of yellow terry cloth, 60 inches wide

Assorted coordinating print fabrics, enough for an 11 x 11 x 15½-inch triangle and a 2 x 20-inch border strip

Fusible web

Print fabric with two 3-inch critter or bug motifs

Coordinating cotton embroidery floss

8 buttons in assorted sizes and pastel colors

Circular template (dinner plate)

Bias binding, 2½ x 150 inches

WHAT YOU DO

1. Cut a 34-inch square and a 13½ x 13½ x 19¼-inch triangle from the yellow terry cloth.

2. Cut an 11 x 11 x 15½-inch triangle from the print fabric and a 2 x 20-inch border strip from a coordinating piece of fabric. To sew the border strip onto the 15½-inch side of the triangle, match up the centers and use a ¼-inch seam allowance (see figure 1). Then trim the excess fabric along the sides of the border strip. Note: To save time, you can omit the border strip and cut a triangle from the print fabric that is the same size as the terry cloth triangle.

3. Apply the fusible web onto the critter print fabric, and cut out two critter images so that they are approximately 3 inches square. Then fuse the two images onto the right side of the print fabric triangle (see Fusible Web Appliqué, page 12).

4. Straight stitch around the motifs using two strands of the coordinating floss. Stitch the buttons as desired.

5. With the edges aligned, pin the two triangles right sides together. Using a ¼-inch seam allowance, sew the triangles along the diagonal side to make a square shape, then press the seam and trim the excess fabric.

6. Press the square back into a triangle along the seam with wrong sides together. Pin the hood onto one corner of the terry cloth square, matching the raw edges.

7. Use a circular template (such as a plate) to round all corners.

8. Machine baste the hood onto the square.

9. To finish the towel, use a ready-made bias binding, or cut and sew your own 2½-inch binding strips using your preferred binding technique. Keep in mind that, because of the rounded corners, it's best to cut your strips on the bias of the fabric (usually 45°) so the binding has more stretch.

tip

The hood of this bath towel is the perfect size for an older toddler or small child. However, if you wish to make one for a newborn, simply adjust the size of the hood to a triangle approximately 10 x 10 x 14 inches. Adjust the size accordingly if you are adding a border strip.

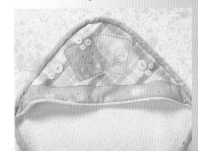

Dirty Duds Cow Laundry Bag

This cute cow will help you hide those dirty duds until laundry day. A combination of machine sewing and embroidery make this darling drawstring bag "udderly" easy to put together. As a fun variation for older tots, this barnyard buddy can be used as a toy or sleep-over pajama bag.

WHAT YOU NEED

Basic materials, tools, and equipment (page 17)

Piece of white fleece, 18 x 60 inches

Cow bag template (page 132)

Felt or wool felt scraps in pink and black

Cotton embroidery floss in black and white

Jumbo safety pin

Piece of white cord, 60 inches

WHAT YOU DO

1. Fold the white fleece in half so you have a piece that is 18 x 30 inches. Make sure that the folded edge of the fleece is facing the bottom.

2. Use the cow bag template on page 132 to trace and cut out one muzzle and two inner ear pieces from the pink felt, and two ears and six spots from the black felt.

3. Using the photo or template for placement, baste the muzzle, ear pieces, and spots onto the folded piece of fleece. Once the felt pieces are basted in the desired position, you can lay the piece of fleece flat for stitching.

4. Blanket-stitch around the ears and spots using two strands of the white floss, and around the muzzle and inner ear pieces using two strands of the black floss.

5. Trace, then back-stitch the mouth using two strands of the black floss. Satin stitch the two nostrils. Then stitch two French knots for the eyes with the black floss.

6. With the edges aligned, pin the fleece in half right sides together.

7. Leaving the top side open, sew along the two sides using a ⅜-inch seam allowance.

8. To make the casing, fold the top of the bag over approximately 1½ to 1¾ inches. Pin the fold and sew along the bottom edge of it, then turn the bag right side out.

9. Cut a small slit in the front center of the casing seam (through the top layer of fleece only). Using a jumbo safety pin, thread one end of the cord into the opening, then string the length of the cord through the casing. Tie a knot at each end and separate the strands to make a tassel.

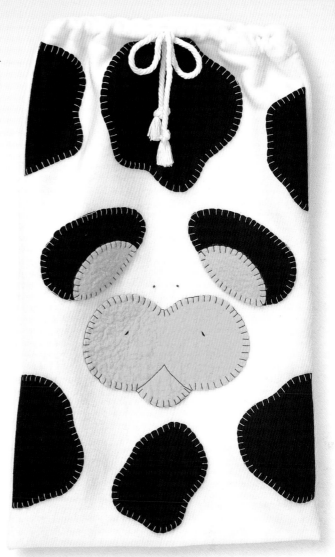

Rub-A-Dub-Dub Bath Bag

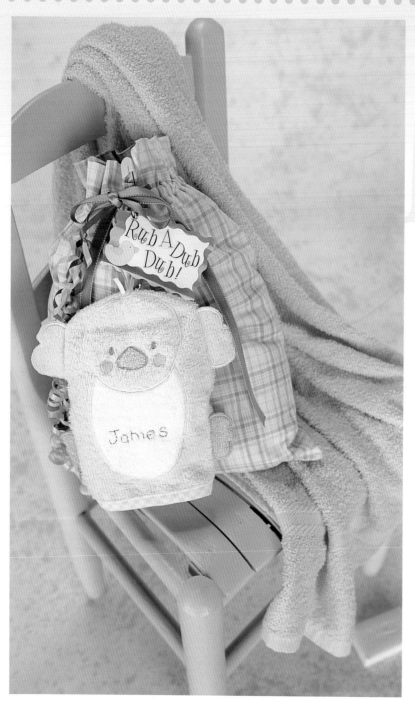

Need a last-minute shower gift? You can stitch up this delightful bath bag in no time, then fill it with a selection of store-bought bath toys and accessories. For a personalized touch, embroider an inexpensive bath mitt with the child's name, then add a coordinating gift tag. Mom can use the bag to store bath toys or other bathing essentials.

WHAT YOU NEED

Basic materials, tools, and equipment (page 17)

Piece of blue and green plaid print fabric, 22 x 18 inches

Safety pin

Ribbon to match fabric, 3/8 x 40 inches

Duck bath mitt

Blue cotton embroidery floss

Washcloths and assorted bath products

3 diaper pins (optional)

To make the gift tag:

White cardstock

Glue stick

Decorative paper

Duck sticker

Alphabet stickers

Decorative-edge scissors

Hole punch

Curling ribbon

WHAT YOU DO

1. With the right sides together, fold the piece of plaid fabric in half so that you have a piece that is 11 x 18 inches, then pin the fabric to secure it.

2. Using a 1/4-inch seam allowance, sew across the bottom and across the long side to make the bag.

3. To make the casing, place the fabric wrong side up on the ironing board, fold the top edge over approximately 1/2 inch, and press it with the iron. Then fold the piece again approximately 1 1/2 inches, and press it.

4. Sew along the pressed edge approximately 1/8 to 1/4 inch from the fold, then sew again about 1 inch from this sewn line.

5. Trim the corners of the bag, turn it, and press it.

6. Cut a small slit in the front center of the casing seam, cutting through the top layer of the fabric only. Using the safety pin, thread one end of the ribbon into the opening, then string the length of ribbon through the casing.

7. If you like, you can personalize the bath mitt with your child's name. Backstitch the name using three strands of the blue floss. With a few stitches, secure the top of the

bath mitt to the front of the bag. Insert the washcloths into the bath mitt, then add three diaper pins along the bottom of the bag for a decorative touch.

8. To make a coordinating gift card, use the decorative paper and the cardstock. Add the duck sticker, then use the alphabet stickers to spell Rub-A-Dub-Dub. To give the card fancy edges, use the decorative-edge scissors when you cut the paper and the cardstock. Punch a hole in the top left corner, then tie the tag to the bag using the curling ribbon.

9. Fill the bag with an assortment of bath products, like soaps, baby powder, bath toys, and washcloths.

CHAPTER FOUR

Discover & Play

TOYS FOR FUN AND ACTIVE LEARNING

It's a joy to watch children discover and explore the world around them. For babies, each new sight and sound equals a wonderful learning adventure. Brimming with fun educational ideas, our toy chest features friendly frog and lion rattles and fleecy barnyard blocks that are perfect for little hands just beginning to grasp and squeeze. And what tot wouldn't love our pocket bunny activity blanket that's full of secret compartments? We've also included two soft learning books that will introduce young minds to the joy of reading. Who knew learning could be so much fun?

Ocean Friends Activity Mat

Take your tot on a learning adventure deep beneath the sea. These cheery ocean critters will teach your child how to match fun shapes and colors while developing basic motor skills. Hand-stitched with felt, the lightweight mat can be rolled up for on-the-go fun. Older tots can use the mat to act out all sorts of imaginary underwater adventures.

WHAT YOU NEED

Basic materials, tools, and equipment (page 17)

Sand, coral, octopus, eel, starfish, clam, fish, and crab templates (page 133)

Scraps of felt in pale green, gray, purple, gold, antique white, aqua, deep rose, and white

Piece of tan felt, 28 x 12 inches

2 pieces of blue felt, each 28 x 22 inches

Cotton embroidery floss in black and ecru

Heavyweight fusible web

Regular-weight fusible web

Hook-and-loop fastener tape, ¾ inch wide

Note: You'll be tracing and cutting out of felt three of each of the shapes. One of each of the shapes will be permanently adhered to the mat using the heavyweight fusible web, while the other two will be stitched together for the matching removable top piece, using the regular-weight fusible web.

WHAT YOU DO

1. Use the Ocean Friends templates on page 133 to trace and cut out the sand bottom from the tan felt and the coral from the pale green felt.

2. With the straight edges aligned, position the sand at the bottom of one of the blue felt pieces. Use the photo or template for placement and position the coral piece so that the bottom edge lies slightly underneath the top of the sand. Then baste the sand and coral shapes.

3. Blanket-stitch around the coral and along the top edge of the sand, using two strands of the black floss.

4. For the permanently adhered bottom shapes, refer to Fusible Web Appliqué, on page 12, then trace and cut out the Ocean Friends templates on page 133 using the heavyweight fusible web and the felt fabrics as follows: octopus (gray), eel (purple), starfish (gold), clam (antique white), fish (aqua), and crab (deep rose). Use the photo or template for placement, and fuse the six critter shapes onto the mat. Then stitch a small piece of the hook-and-loop tape onto the center of each felt shape.

5. For the six top matching shapes, trace and cut out two of each of the Ocean Friends templates from the felt colors listed above. (Although optional, I cut one piece directly from the felt and the other from the same color of felt that has been fused with the regular-weight fusible web. By fusing one of the layers with the webbing, the shape will have more stiffness and will be less likely to stretch out of shape.)

6. Stitch the matching hook-and-loop tape onto the backs of one of the pieces, making sure that they are aligned with the hook-and-loop tape on the bottom shapes.

7. Trace and cut out the 10 eye shapes from the white felt, the five purple spots for the octopus, the three pale green spots for the eel, and the three gold spots for the fish.

8. Using the photo or template for placement, baste the eyes and the spots onto the top pieces, then stitch a French knot in the center of each eye with the black floss.

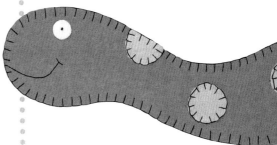

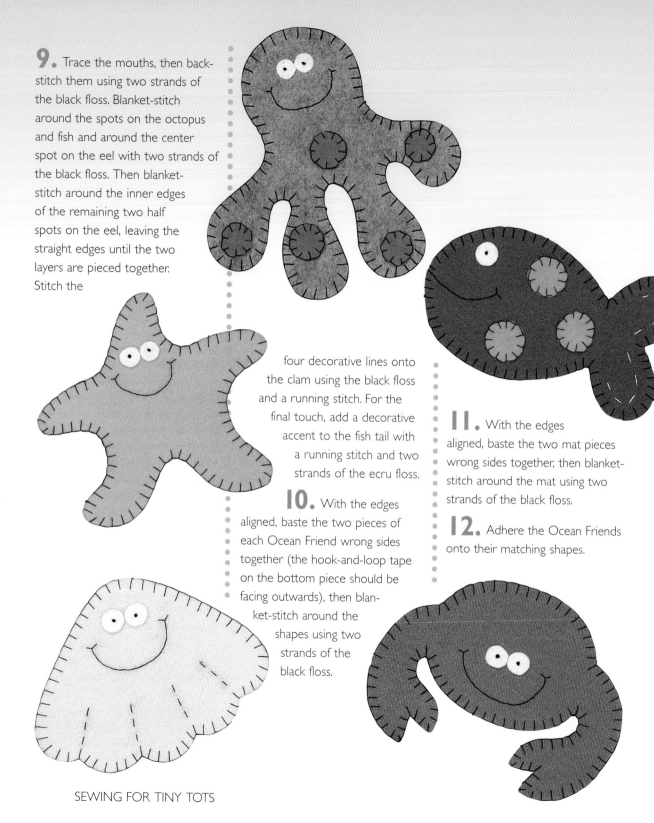

9. Trace the mouths, then back-stitch them using two strands of the black floss. Blanket-stitch around the spots on the octopus and fish and around the center spot on the eel with two strands of the black floss. Then blanket-stitch around the inner edges of the remaining two half spots on the eel, leaving the straight edges until the two layers are pieced together. Stitch the four decorative lines onto the clam using the black floss and a running stitch. For the final touch, add a decorative accent to the fish tail with a running stitch and two strands of the ecru floss.

10. With the edges aligned, baste the two pieces of each Ocean Friend wrong sides together (the hook-and-loop tape on the bottom piece should be facing outwards), then blanket-stitch around the shapes using two strands of the black floss.

11. With the edges aligned, baste the two mat pieces wrong sides together, then blanket-stitch around the mat using two strands of the black floss.

12. Adhere the Ocean Friends onto their matching shapes.

Jungle Friends Pacifier Pals, Puppets, and Rattle

To make the pacifier pals:

WHAT YOU NEED

Basic materials, tools, and equipment (page 17)

Lion, elephant, and monkey head templates (page 133)

Scraps of felt in tan, cream, gray, pink, and brown

Cotton embroidery floss in dark brown, black, pink, and beige

Polyester fiberfill

Pacifiers

Round hook-and-loop fasteners, ⅜ inch diameter

WHAT YOU DO

1. Use the Jungle Friends templates on page 133 to trace and cut out two lion heads from the tan felt, a lion face from the cream felt, two elephant heads from the gray felt, two cheeks from the pink felt, two monkey heads from the brown felt, and a monkey face from the cream felt.

2. Referring to the photo or template for placement, baste the lion face onto the center of one of the lion head pieces. Blanket stitch around the face using two strands of the dark brown floss. Then satin stitch the nose using two strands of the pink floss. Trace the mouth, then backstitch it using two strands of the brown floss. Add two brown French knots for the eyes and three straight stitches on each side of the face for the whiskers.

3. With the edges aligned, place the two lion head pieces wrong sides together, and blanket-stitch around the head using two strands of the brown floss, leaving an opening wide enough for stuffing. Stuff the head with polyester fiberfill, then blanket-stitch the opening closed.

4. Baste the two cheeks onto one of the elephant head pieces, then blanket stitch around the cheeks using two strands of the black floss. Add two black French knots for the eyes.

5. With the edges aligned, place the two elephant head pieces wrong sides together, and blanket-stitch around the head with two strands of the black floss, leaving an opening wide enough at the top for stuffing. Stuff the head with polyester fiberfill, then blanket-stitch the opening closed.

6. Baste the monkey face onto one of the monkey head pieces, then blanket-stitch around the top part of the face using two strands of the beige floss. (The outer edge of the face will be stitched when the monkey heads are pieced together.) Trace the mouth, then backstitch it using two strands of the dark brown floss. Add two brown French knots for the eyes. Using two strands of the pink floss, satin stitch the two nostrils and the inside of the ears.

7. With the edges aligned, place the two monkey head pieces wrong sides together, and blanket-stitch around the head with two strands of the beige floss, leaving an opening wide enough for stuffing. Stuff the head with polyester fiberfill, then blanket-stitch the opening closed.

8. For each pacifier pal, cut a 1 x 6-inch strip out of matching felt with pinking shears. Stitch one end of the strip onto the back of each head, then adhere the hook-and-loop fasteners onto the ends of each strip and insert a pacifier onto the loop.

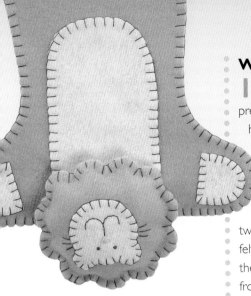

WHAT YOU DO

1. Refer to steps 1 to 5 on the previous page to make a felt lion head and a felt elephant head.

2. Use the puppet template on page 133 to trace and cut out two puppet shapes from the tan felt and two puppet shapes from the gray felt. For the lion, trace and cut out the two paws and the belly shape from the cream felt.

3. Referring to the photo or template for placement, baste the lion paws and the belly shape onto one of the tan puppet pieces. Blanket-stitch around the paws and the inner edges of the belly, using two strands of the dark brown floss. Be sure to leave the top straight edge of the belly unstitched until the two layers are pieced together.

4. Stitch the lion and elephant heads onto the front of one of the puppet pieces. For the lion, this will be the piece with the paws and belly.

5. Pin the puppet pieces wrong sides together. Trim the bottom straight edge of each puppet with pinking shears.

6. Leaving the bottom edge open, blanket-stitch around the puppet shape, using two strands of the brown floss for the lion and two strands of the black floss for the elephant.

To make the puppets:

WHAT YOU NEED

Basic materials, tools, and equipment (page 17)

Lion and elephant head templates (page 133)

Puppet body template (page 133)

Scraps of felt in tan, gray, cream, and pink

Cotton embroidery floss in dark brown, pink, and black

Polyester fiberfill

To make the rattle:

WHAT YOU NEED

Basic materials, tools and equipment (page 17)

Lion head template (page 133)

Ribbit frog rattle handle template (page 132)

Scraps of tan and cream felt

Cotton embroidery floss in dark brown and pink

Polyester fiberfill

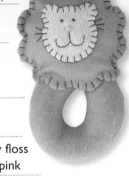

WHAT YOU DO

1. To make the felt lion head, follow the instructions on the previous page (Jungle Friends Pacifier Pals).

2. Use the frog rattle template on page 132 to trace and cut out two rattle handle shapes from the tan felt.

3. With the edges aligned, pin the two handle shapes together. Using a ¼-inch seam allowance, sew the two pieces together, leaving one end open, then turn the handle right side out.

4. Stuff the handle with polyester fiberfill. Overlap the two end pieces, then slip stitch the opening closed, while at the same time stitching the two end pieces together. Then stitch the handle onto the back of the lion's head.

SEWING FOR TINY TOTS

Wiggly Worm Play Pal

Kids of all ages will go buggy over this creepy crawly critter. A perfect playmate, this lovable, huggable character is easy to make using soft fleece fabric and scraps of colorful felt. With his cheery smile, yellow button nose and rosy pink cheeks, he's sure to wiggle his way into your child's heart.

WHAT YOU NEED

Basic materials, tools, and equipment (page 17)

Worm template (page 132)

⅔ yard of lime green fleece

Scraps of pink and yellow felt or wool felt

Black cotton embroidery floss

Polyester fiberfill

WHAT YOU DO

1. Use the Wiggly Worm template on page 132 to trace and cut out two worm shapes from the lime green fleece, two cheeks from the pink felt, and the nose from the yellow felt.

2. Referring to the photo or template for placement, baste the two cheeks and the nose shape onto one of the worm pieces.

3. Blanket-stitch around the cheeks and nose, using two strands of the black floss.

4. Trace the mouth, then back-stitch it using two strands of the black floss. Stitch black French knots for the eyes, then sew a single straight stitch above each eye for the eyebrows. Using a running stitch and two strands of the black floss, add six decorative stripes onto the body of the worm.

5. With the edges aligned, pin the two worm pieces wrong sides together, then blanket-stitch around the worm with two strands of the black floss, leaving an opening wide enough in the center for stuffing.

6. Stuff the worm with polyester fiberfill, then blanket-stitch the opening closed.

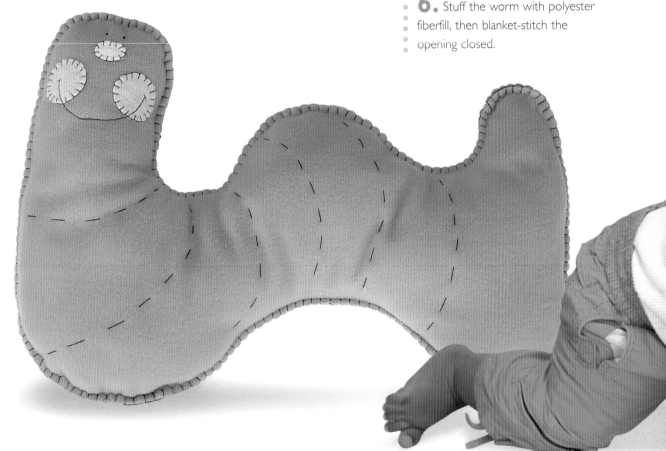

Ribbit Frog Rattle

This fun frog rattle is guaranteed to please even the tiniest tadpoles in the pond. Fashioned from soft fleece with embroidered felt details, he's ideal for little hands to grasp and squeeze.

WHAT YOU NEED

Basic materials, tools, and equipment (page 17)

Frog rattle template (page 132)

Scraps of lime green fleece

Scraps of pink and cream felt

Black cotton embroidery floss

Polyester fiberfill

WHAT YOU DO

1. Use the frog rattle template on page 132 to trace and cut out two frog heads and two handle shapes from the lime green fleece, two cheeks from the pink felt, and two eyes from the cream felt.

2. Referring to the photo or template for placement, baste the two cheeks and eyes onto one of the frog head pieces. When positioning the pieces, remember to allow a ¼-inch seam allowance around the edges.

3. Blanket-stitch around the cheeks, using two strands of the black floss. Trace the mouth, then backstitch it using two strands of the black floss. Add two straight stitches for the nostrils and a black French knot in the center of each eye. Then sew three tiny running stitches onto the top of each eye.

4. With the edges aligned, pin the two frog head pieces right sides together. Using a ¼-inch seam allowance, sew the two pieces together, leaving an opening wide enough at the bottom for stuffing.

5. Trim the corners, then turn the head right side out. Stuff the head with polyester fiberfill, and slip stitch the opening closed.

6. With the edges aligned, pin the two handle shapes together. Using a ¼-inch seam allowance, sew the two pieces together, leaving one end open.

7. Turn the handle right side out and stuff it with polyester fiberfill. Overlap the two end pieces, then slip stitch the opening closed, while at the same time stitching the two end pieces together. Stitch the handle onto the back of the frog's head.

Barnyard Buddy Blocks

Round up this delightful trio of farmyard friends for hours of playtime fun. Made from pretty pastel fleece and felt in an array of colors, these soft, squishy barnyard blocks are irresistibly cute when adorned with lamb, pig, and chick motifs. With the added bonus of polka-dots, the blocks can also be used as a basic counting game.

WHAT YOU NEED

Basic materials, tools, and equipment (page 17)

Lamb, pig, chick, and polka-dot templates (page 135)

Scraps of fleece in cream, pink, and yellow

Scraps of felt in dark gray, bright pink, and orange

Six 8-inch squares of assorted pastel fleece for each block (or a total of 18 for the three blocks), plus scraps for the polka dots (Note: For the lamb block I use pink (front), yellow (top), cream (bottom), blue and cream (sides), and green (back); for the pig block I use yellow (front and back), blue (top and bottom), and pink and green (sides); for the chick block I use blue (front), pink (top and bottom), cream and green (sides), and yellow (back).

Cotton embroidery floss in bright pink, yellow, ecru, pale blue, and a medium blue

Polyester fiberfill

WHAT YOU DO

1. Use the barnyard buddy templates on page 135 to trace and cut out the lamb, pig, and chick motifs as follows: lamb's body (cream fleece) and lamb's head and legs (dark gray felt), pig's head (pink fleece) and pig's snout (bright pink felt), chick's body and wings (yellow fleece) and beak (orange felt).

2. Using the same template on page 135, trace and cut out the polka dots from scraps of the assorted colors of fleece. (I use a total of six dots for each block, which are applied in groupings of one, two, and three on the top and two sides. I left the back and bottom sides blank.) Feel free to cut additional dots if you want to cover all sides of the blocks (like dice). You can then add combinations of four and five dot patterns.

(Tip: The blocks can be rolled like dice and used as a counting game for older tots.)

3. Use the photo or template for placement to baste the barnyard buddy motifs onto the desired color fleece square. Note: I basted the lamb onto a pink square, the pig onto a yellow square, and the chick onto a blue square.

4. Baste the polka dots onto the remaining fleece squares as desired. For visual interest, try varying your dot patterns so that each block is different.

5. Blanket-stitch around the lamb's body, using two strands of the medium blue floss, and around the head and legs with two strands of the ecru floss. Use two strands of the pink floss to satin stitch the nose, backstitch inside the ears, and backstitch a small line running down from the center of the nose. Stitch two pale blue French knots for the eyes.

6. Blanket-stitch around the pig's head, using two strands of the medium blue floss, and around the snout using two strands of the yellow floss. Add two cross-stitches for the nostrils, using two strands of the ecru floss. Backstitch inside the ears with two strands of the pink floss. Then stitch two pale blue French knots for the eyes.

To assemble the blocks:

9. With right sides together and using a ⅜-inch seam allowance, sew four of the squares together end to end. (Tip: For variety, place contrasting colors next to one another.) Sew the two ends together to make an open box.

10. With right sides facing, pin the fifth square onto the top opening of the block, then sew around all four sides. Repeat for the bottom using the sixth square. Be sure to leave one side open for turning and stuffing.

11. Trim the corners, turn the piece right side out, and stuff it tightly with polyester fiberfill. Then slip stitch the opening closed.

7. For the chick, blanket-stitch around the body and wings, using two strands of the pink floss, and around the beak with two strands of the ecru floss. Stitch two pale blue French knots for the eyes. For the buttons, add three cross-stitches using two strands of the medium blue floss.

8. Use two strands of contrasting floss to blanket-stitch around the dots as desired.

Pocket Bunny Activity Blanket

This cuddly fleece activity blanket is sure to inspire hours of imaginative play. Baby will be delighted if you attach a toy to each of the colorful rickrack loops and tuck one in each of the bunny pockets. The blanket is also lightweight and portable, a bonus for on-the-go moms and babies.

WHAT YOU NEED

Basic materials, tools, and equipment (page 17)

1¼ yards of cream fleece

⅜ yard of pink fleece

⅜ yard of blue fleece

⅜ yard of yellow fleece

Bunny pocket, ear, and polka-dot templates (page 131)

5 pink buttons

Cotton embroidery floss in pastel pink, green, yellow, and blue

28 inches of jumbo yellow chenille rickrack

4 plastic attachment clips or rings

A variety of toys, plush animals, rattles, teething rings, etc. (to attach onto clips and insert into pockets)

WHAT YOU DO

1. Cut nine 12-inch squares of fleece. (I use four cream, two pink, two blue, and one yellow so the blanket will suit either a baby boy or girl.)

2. Cut five 6 x 7-inch pieces of cream fleece for the bunny pockets. Pin the top edge of each pocket over approximately 1 inch to create a cuff (you'll be left with a 6-inch square). Then sew approximately ¼ inch from the bottom edge of the cuff.

3. Referring to the photo or template on page 131 for placement, stitch the five pink buttons for the

noses. Trace the mouth, then back-stitch it on each pocket using two strands of the pink floss. Stitch two blue French knots for the eyes.

4. Use the bunny ear template on page 131 to trace and cut out 10 ear shapes from the cream fleece, then stitch the ears onto the back of each pocket.

5. Pin a bunny pocket onto the center of each of the five colored squares of fleece. Using a ¼- to ⅜-inch seam allowance, sew along the sides and bottom of each pocket (leaving the top side open). For a decorative touch, blanket-stitch around the pocket using two strands of coordinating floss. (Note: Be careful not to stitch the top of the pocket closed.)

6. Use the circle template on page 131 to trace and cut out twelve polka dots (four each from the pink, blue, and yellow fleece). Baste one pink, one blue, and one yellow dot onto each of the four cream fleece squares, then blanket-stitch around the dots using two strands of floss as follows: yellow (blue dots), blue (pink dots), and pink (yellow dots).

7. To assemble the blanket, refer to the Piecing a Quilt or Blanket section on page 12. Sew the first row so that the pink and blue squares are on the left and right, and the cream square is in the center. Alternate the second row so

that the cream squares are on the left and right, and the yellow square is in the center. Sew the third row in the same manner as the first, but alternate the position of the blue and pink squares.

8. Cut four 7-inch pieces of the yellow rickrack, form a loop with each piece, then stitch the ends onto the top center of each of the four cream squares.

9. With the seams aligned, sew the first and second rows together, then sew the third row to complete the top of the blanket.

10. Measure the length and width of the blanket, then cut a piece of cream fleece that's the same size to serve as the backing.

11. With the edges aligned, pin the two blanket pieces right sides together.

12. Sew around the edges of the blanket, leaving an opening wide enough at the bottom for turning. Trim the corners, then turn the blanket right side out. Slip stitch the opening closed.

13. Attach the four plastic clips to the rickrack loops, and use them to hang a variety of toys, rattles, and teething rings from the blanket. Tuck a toy or plush animal into each of the bunny pockets for extra fun!

If the blanket is being made specifically for a baby boy or girl, you can cut costs by making a two-tone blanket, alternating the cream fleece with one other color, like pink or blue. Since fleece is generally sold in 60-inch widths, you'll get more usage out of the width of the fabric.

What's in My Pocket? Activity Book

These bright and colorful pocket pals are the perfect way to introduce your tot to the joy of books. The cheery pages encourage the development of basic motor skills while teaching important visual concepts such as colors and shapes. Little hands will love turning the pages to see what "peek-a-boo" surprise lies next.

WHAT YOU NEED

Basic materials, tools, and equipment (page 17)

Pocket template (use one from Keepsake Book, page 134)

Fish, crown, flower, bear, and duck templates (page 134)

Scraps of felt in purple, aqua, fuchsia, gold, yellow, pale green, brown, tan, pale blue, and black

Cotton embroidery floss in yellow, fuchsia, black, ecru, purple, dark brown, orange, and aqua blue (or a matching color for the binding)

6 pieces of cream felt, 9 x 9 inches

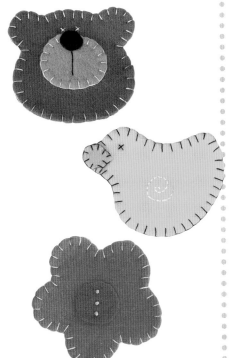

WHAT YOU DO

1. Use the pocket book template on page 134 to trace and cut out five pocket shapes. Cut one shape each out of the purple, fuchsia, yellow, pale green, and pale blue felt.

2. Trace and cut out the felt motifs as follows: fish (three fish shapes out of the aqua felt and two cheeks from the fuchsia felt), crown (three crown shapes out of the gold felt and six small circles from the purple felt), flower (three flower shapes out of the fuchsia felt and two circular centers from the purple felt), bear (three bear head shapes out of the brown felt, two muzzles out of the tan felt, and two noses from the black felt), duck (three duck shapes out of the yellow felt and two beaks from the gold felt).

To make the pockets:

3. Baste one of the felt motifs onto each of the five pockets as follows: fish (purple pocket), crown (fuchsia pocket), flower (yellow pocket), bear (pale green pocket), and duck (pale blue pocket).

4. Using the template or photo for placement, baste a cheek onto one of the fish, three of the decorative circles onto the crown, a circular center onto one of the flowers, a muzzle and a nose onto the bear, and a beak onto the duck.

5. Blanket-stitch around the fish, using two strands of the fuchsia floss. Then use two strands of the yellow floss to straight stitch around the cheek, and add three decorative lines to the tail. Trace the mouth, then backstitch it using two strands of the black floss. Stitch a small black cross-stitch for the eye.

6. Blanket-stitch around the crown, using two strands of the black floss. Add a yellow French knot onto the center of each of the three purple circles.

7. Blanket-stitch around the flower using two strands of the ecru floss, then add three yellow French knots vertically along the center of the purple circle.

8. Blanket-stitch around the bear head and muzzle, using two strands of the ecru floss. Add two small ecru cross-stitches for the eyes. Stitch around the nose to secure it, using two strands of the black floss, then backstitch a small line running down the center of the nose.

9. Blanket-stitch around the duck and beak, using two strands of the black floss, then add a small black cross-stitch for the eye. Use three strands of the ecru floss to back-stitch a decorative swirl for the wing.

10. Blanket-stitch along the top straight edge of each pocket (where the pocket will remain open), using two strands of floss as follows: fish pocket (yellow floss), crown pocket (ecru floss), flower pocket (purple floss), bear pocket (brown floss), and duck pocket (orange floss). You will complete the blanket stitch around the pocket in the next step.

11. Pin each pocket onto one of the felt squares, then continue to blanket-stitch around the pocket so that the stitches join the ones already in place along the straight (open) edge.

To make the matching shapes:

12. To complete the matching shapes that tuck inside the pockets, follow steps 4 to 9, but blanket-stitch around each shape after you stitch the front accents. Once you've added the decorative details to the front of each piece, baste the two layers together, then blanket-stitch around the outer edges as a final step.

To assemble the book:

13. Choose one pocket page for the cover (I chose the fish), then pin this cover page to another page of your choice (I chose the crown) wrong sides together. Pin two more

of the pocket pages (I chose the flower and bear) wrong sides together, then pin the final pocket page (mine is the duck) onto the remaining blank felt square (this one will be the back cover of the book).

14. Using a ½-inch seam allowance, sew along the top, right side, and bottom of each of the pinned pages, leaving the left side (or spine) open.

15. Using pinking shears, trim along the three sewn edges of each page.

16. With the edges aligned, stack the three sewn pages together, making sure that you have the desired layout for your book (the back cover should be blank).

17. Using six strands of the aqua blue floss (or a matching color if using a different cover motif), use large blanket stitches to bind the pages together along the left side of the book.

Sweet Treats Counting Book

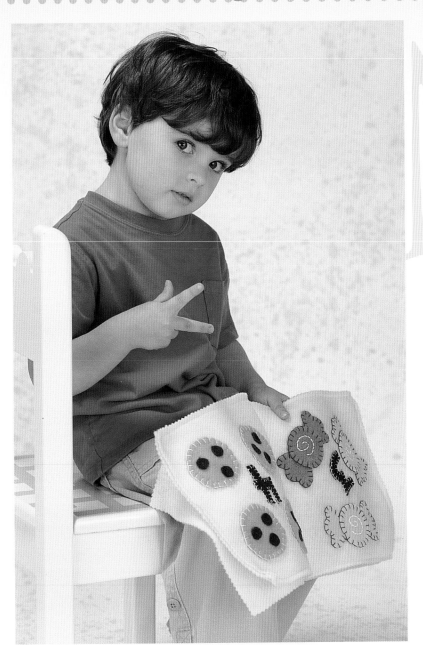

Make learning fun with this yummy first counting book. Each page has its own delectable discovery, from cherry-topped sundaes and ice cream cones to gooey gumdrops and melt-in-your-mouth cookies. Learning to count has never been so deliciously fun.

WHAT YOU NEED

Basic materials, tools, and equipment (page 17)

Sundae, ice cream cone, donut, peppermint, cookie, and gumdrop templates (page 135)

Number templates (same as Counting Sheep Wall Quilt, page 127)

Scraps of felt in dark brown, gray, white, brown, pink, tan, pale green, purple, blue, and yellow

9 inches of pink, white, and green candy stripe ribbon, ⅝ inch wide

Iron-on adhesive hem or fusible web tape, ⅝ inch wide

7 pieces of cream felt, 9 inches square

Cotton embroidery floss in dark brown and ecru

WHAT YOU DO

1. Use the Sweet Treats templates on page 135 and the Counting Sheep number templates on page 127 to trace and cut out the felt motifs as follows: numbers (two ones, two twos, two threes, one four, and one five out of the dark brown felt); sundae (bowl out of the gray felt, ice cream out of the white felt, chocolate sauce out of the brown felt, and a cherry from the pink felt); ice cream cone (cone out of the tan felt, ice cream scoop out of the white felt, and a cherry from the pink felt); two donuts out of the tan felt; three peppermints out of the pale green, pink, and purple felt; cookies (four cookie shapes out of the tan felt and 12 chocolate pieces from the dark brown felt); and gumdrops (five gumdrops out of the blue, purple, yellow, pink, and pale green felt, and five icing trims from the white felt).

2. Cut a 5⅛-inch piece and a 3-inch piece of the candy stripe ribbon. Then cut a 5⅛-inch piece and a 3-inch piece of the adhesive hem or fusible tape. Following the manufacturer's instructions, apply the adhesive hem or fusible tape onto the ribbon pieces. Then trim the ends of the ribbon pieces at a slight angle so that they align with the edges of the sundae bowl and ice cream cone. Adhere the 5⅛-inch piece of ribbon to the bowl and the 3-inch piece to the cone.

3. Referring to the templates and photos for placement, baste the sundae and numbers 1, 2, and 3 onto one of the felt squares for the cover page. Then baste the ice cream cone and a 1 onto the first page, the two donuts and a 2 onto the second page, the three peppermints and a 3 onto the third page, the four cookies and a 4 onto the fourth page, and the five gumdrops and a 5 onto the fifth page. The remaining blank felt square will serve as the back cover.

4. Blanket-stitch around the sundae bowl, the ice cream, and the cherry using two strands of the dark brown floss, and around the chocolate sauce and three numbers using two strands of the ecru floss.

5. Blanket-stitch around the entire ice cream cone, using two strands of the dark brown floss, and around the number 1, using two strands of the ecru floss.

6. Blanket-stitch around the two donuts, using two strands of the dark brown floss, and around the number 2, using two strands of the ecru floss.

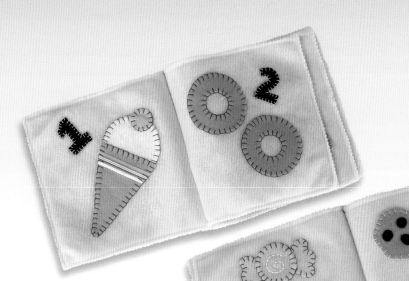

7. Blanket-stitch around the three peppermints, using two strands of the dark brown floss, and around the number 3, using two strands of the ecru floss. Then use three strands of the ecru floss to stitch a decorative swirl in the center of each peppermint.

8. Blanket-stitch around the four cookies and around the number 4, using two strands of the ecru floss. Using two strands of the dark brown floss, add cross stitches in the center of the chocolate pieces to secure them.

9. Blanket-stitch around the five gumdrops, using two strands of the dark brown floss, and around the number 5, using two strands of the ecru floss.

To assemble the book:

10. Pin the sundae cover page to the ice cream cone page, wrong sides together, then pin the two donuts and three peppermints pages wrong sides together. Finally, pin the four cookies and five gumdrops pages wrong sides together.

11. Using a ½-inch seam allowance, sew along the top, right side, and bottom of each of the pinned pages, leaving the left side (or spine) open. When sewing the pinned pages, you will have the sun-dae cover, the two donuts and the four cookies facing upwards.

12. Use pinking shears to trim along the three sewn edges of each page. Then use the pinking shears to trim the remaining blank felt square along the same three edges so it's the same size as the other pages.

13. With the edges aligned, stack the three sewn pages and the back cover together, making sure that you have the pages in sequential order.

14. Sew large blanket stitches with six strands of the dark brown floss to bind the pages together along the left side (or spine) of the book.

CHAPTER FIVE

Hugs & Heartstrings

PRECIOUS KEEPSAKES AND MEMORY CRAFTS

You've captured those wonderful baby moments on film. Now what? In this chapter, we'll show you how to preserve and display your favorite photos in creative ways that go beyond the typical store-bought picture frame or scrapbook. With our easy photo transferring technique, you can print cherished images onto fabric, then use the fabric-printed photos to personalize quilts, pillows, memory books, diaper bags, and more. We'll also inspire you with other fresh ideas for preserving special memories, including stamping Baby's footprints and creative journaling with simple embroidery stitches.

Jane Marie

June 17, 2006

Keepsake Birth Pillow

Adorned with delicate embroidery, dainty pink flowers, and romantic ribbon trims, this keepsake pillow is simply heavenly. Perfect as a gift, this timeless treasure is stitched entirely by hand and personalized with Baby's name, photo, and date of birth.

WHAT YOU NEED

Basic materials, tools, and equipment (page 17)

Pillow template (page 134)

2 pieces of cream wool felt, each 13 x 9 inches

14 chenille flowers, each ¾ inch (I use five fuchsia, five pink, and four cream)

4 pieces of green ribbon, each ⅛ x 9 inches

14 pink pearl beads, 6 mm diameter

5 x 3½-inch photo (Note: A black-and-white or sepia-tone photo adds to the nostalgic charm of the pillow.)

Self-adhesive plastic photo sleeve (Note: I trimmed a 4 x 6-inch photo sleeve to fit a 5 x 3½-inch photo.)

Hot glue and hot-glue gun

Cotton embroidery floss in pink and green

18 inches of pink and green lace flower trim, ⅜ inch wide

4 pink ribbon rosebuds with flat green bows, each 1-inch wide

Polyester fiberfill

WHAT YOU DO

1. Use the pillow template on page 134 to trace and cut out two pillow shapes from the cream felt.

2. Stitch a chenille flower (alternating between the fuchsia, pink and cream) onto the scalloped edges of one of the pillow pieces.

3. Tie four bows with the green ribbon, then stitch each of the four bows onto a corner of the pillow.

4. Stitch the pink beads around the edge of the pillow in between the chenille flower trims.

5. Insert the photo into the photo sleeve, then stitch (or hot glue) the sleeve onto the center of the pillow top.

6. Trace the name so that it's centered above the photo, then trace the date of birth underneath the photo. Backstitch both, using three strands of the pink floss.

7. Cut two 5¼-inch pieces and two 3¾-inch pieces of the lace flower trim, and glue them around the photo sleeve. Then glue the ribbon rosebuds onto each corner of the photo sleeve.

8. With the edges aligned, pin the two pillow pieces wrong sides together, then blanket-stitch around the pillow with three strands of the green floss, leaving an opening wide enough for stuffing.

9. Stuff the pillow with polyester fiberfill, then blanket-stitch the opening closed.

Mini Jean Pocket Purse

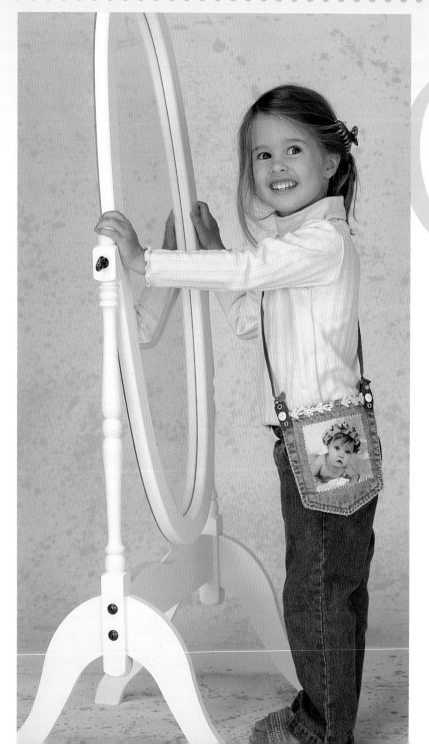

Oh, *what fun clever moms will have recycling their old jean pockets into darling denim purses.* Your one-of-a-kind *creation makes the perfect purse for a big sister who wants to show off her new sibling in style.*

WHAT YOU NEED

Basic materials, tools, and equipment (page 17)

Denim pocket from an old pair of jeans, 7 x 6½ inches (Note: Be sure to cut out both layers of the pocket, not just the front piece.)

Ecru cotton embroidery floss

7 inches of cream lace flower trim, ½ inch wide

Square fabric printed photo, 4 inches (Scrap of heavyweight natural cotton fabric; digital photo, 4 inches square; photo transfer paper, computer, and inkjet printer)

8 inches of denim ribbon, ¾ inch wide (I use a ribbon with pre-punched silver metal eyelets.)

32 inches of denim ribbon, ⅜ inch wide

2 ivory buttons and 1 silver metal button

Hot glue and hot-glue gun

WHAT YOU DO

1. Blanket-stitch around the edges of the denim pocket, using two strands of the ecru floss.

2. Stitch the 7-inch piece of lace flower trim across the top of the pocket.

3. Follow the manufacturer's instructions for the photo transfer paper to transfer the photo onto the piece of cotton fabric, then trim around the photo with pinking shears. (See page 16 for more on photo transfers.)

4. Baste the photo onto the front of the pocket, then straight stitch around it using two strands of the ecru floss.

5. Cut two pieces of the ¾-inch-wide denim ribbon, each 4-inches long, then fold each piece in half and stitch the ends of the pieces onto each side of the pocket.

6. Tie the ends of the ⅜-inch-wide denim ribbon onto the two loops for a strap.

7. Hot glue (or stitch) the three buttons onto the purse, with an ivory button on each ribbon loop and the silver metal button in the center.

Keepsake Memory Quilt

Machine-stitched in soft floral and gingham prints, this vintage-inspired cotton and chenille quilt is simply divine when adorned with delicate ribbon embroidery, an angelic photo, and romantic heart appliqués. To complete the look, craft a coordinating keepsake pillow embellished with a ribbon bow and dainty rosebud trims.

WHAT YOU NEED

Basic materials, tools, and equipment (page 17)

½ yard of pale green floral fabric (for border strips, the 6-inch center square and heart appliqués)

Fusible web

Heart template (page 131) (Use the one on the bunny.)

Assorted print fabric in coordinating peach, pink, and cream tones (4 pieces, each 6 x 6 inches for the corners, and ¼ yard for the binding)

Pink cotton embroidery floss

8 pink ribbon rosebuds with green leaves, each 1 inch wide

Fabric printed photo, 4 x 4¼ inches (Scrap of heavyweight natural cotton fabric; digital photo, 3½ x 3¾; photo transfer paper, computer, and inkjet printer)

5 pieces of pink ribbon, ⅛ x 11 inches

4 pink ribbon rosebuds with green leaves, each 1½ inches wide

4 pieces of cream chenille fabric, each 6 x 6 inches

Green ribbon, ⅛ inch wide (for ribbon embroidery)

Piece of quilt batting, 24 x 24 inches

¾ yard of solid or print fabric (for quilt backing)

2 plastic rings (for hanging)

WHAT YOU DO

1. Cut out a piece of the pale green fabric to fit four heart templates. Apply the fusible web onto the cut fabric piece (see Fusible Web Appliqué, page 12), then trace and cut out four heart shapes. Fuse the heart appliqués onto the center of the four corner squares. Blanket-stitch around the heart shapes, using two strands of the pink floss.

2. Stitch four of the 1-inch pink ribbon rosebuds onto the top center of the heart appliqués.

3. Follow the manufacturer's instructions for the photo transfer paper to transfer the photo onto the piece of natural cotton fabric, then trim around the photo with pinking shears to create a border. (See page 16 for more on using photo transfers.)

4. Baste the photo onto the center square, then sew a running stitch around the edge of the photo using two strands of the pink floss.

5. Stitch the four remaining 1-inch ribbon rosebuds onto each corner of the photo. Tie a bow with one of the pieces of pink ribbon, then stitch the bow onto the bottom center of the photo.

6. Stitch the four 1½-inch pink ribbon rosebuds onto the chenille squares, approximately 2 inches from the top side. To stitch the flower stems and leaves, use the ⅛-inch-wide green ribbon and follow the embroidery techniques shown in the Stitch Guide on page 15. For each of the four flowers, backstitch the stems so that they're 2 inches in length, and add two Lazy Daisy stitches for the leaves. (Note: If you prefer to use the traditional embroidery techniques, just substitute six strands of green floss for the ribbon.)

A great way to use up scraps of fabric is to sew your binding strips together using a variety of prints.

7. Tie four bows with the remaining ⅛-inch-wide pink ribbon pieces, then stitch the bows onto each of the four flowers, just underneath the ribbon rosebuds.

8. Sew the first row of the quilt together so that a chenille square is in the center, and heart squares are on the left side and right side (see Piecing a Quilt or Blanket, page 12). Then sew the second row with the photo square in the center and chenille squares on either side. Sew the final row in the same manner as the first, with heart squares on the left and right sides, and the remaining chenille square in the center.

9. With the seams aligned, sew the first and second rows together, then sew the final row to complete the center block.

10. Measure the length of the quilt top through the center, raw edge to raw edge, then use this measurement to cut two 2½-inch-wide border strips from the pale green floral fabric. Pin the border strips onto each side of the quilt top, then sew them on.

11. Measure the width of the quilt top through the center, raw edge to raw edge, then use this measurement to cut two additional 2½-inch-wide border strips from the pale green floral fabric. Pin and sew the strips onto the top and bottom of the quilt top in the same manner as the side borders.

12. Cut the quilt batting and the solid or print backing fabric slightly larger than the size of the quilt top, then baste the batting in between the top and bottom layers of the quilt, with the wrong sides of the quilt top and the backing fabric facing together.

13. Pin the three layers together, stitch-in-the-ditch along the seams, then trim the backing and the batting so that they're even with the edges of the quilt top.

14. Finish the edges of the quilt using a coordinating fabric and your preferred binding technique. Then stitch two plastic rings onto the back of the quilt for hanging.

Keepsake Memory Pillow

WHAT YOU DO

1. Follow the manufacturer's instructions for the photo transfer paper to transfer the photo onto the piece of natural cotton fabric, then trim around the photo with pinking shears to create a border. (See page 16 for more on using photo transfers.)

2. Baste the photo onto the center of one of the fabric squares, then add a running stitch around the edge of the photo using two strands of the pink floss.

3. Stitch one of the pink ribbon rosebuds onto each corner of the photo. Tie a bow with the pink ribbon, then stitch it onto the bottom center of the photo.

4. With the edges aligned, pin the two fabric squares right sides together. Using a ½-inch seam allowance, sew the squares together leaving an opening wide enough at the bottom to insert the pillow form.

5. Trim the corners, turn the pillow right side out, and insert the pillow form (or you could stuff the entire pillow with polyester fiberfill).

6. Slip stitch the opening closed.

WHAT YOU NEED

Basic materials, tools, and equipment (page 17)

Fabric printed photo, 5¾ x 6¼ inches (Scrap of heavyweight natural cotton fabric; digital photo, 5 x 5½ inches; photo transfer paper, computer, and inkjet printer)

2 pieces of pale green floral fabric, each 12½ x 12½ inches

Pink cotton embroidery floss

Four pink ribbon rosebuds with green leaves, each 1 inch wide

12 inches of pink ribbon, ⅛ inch wide

Pillow form, 12 x 12 inches (or polyester fiberfill)

Special Delivery Tote Bags

What a "picture-perfect" way to announce Baby's arrival. Using fusible web and a simple photo transferring technique, you can create these super-cute favor bags to celebrate a special delivery in style. Fill the bags with tasty treats, then top them off with festive gift tags and curling ribbon.

WHAT YOU NEED

Basic materials, tools, and equipment (page 17)

Natural cotton canvas mini tote bags, 6 x 4½ inches

Scraps of print fabrics, 5 x 5 inches

Fusible web

Fabric printed photos, 2½ x 3¼ inches or 3 inches square (Scraps of heavyweight natural cotton fabric; digital photos, 2½ x 3¼ inches or 3 inches square; photo transfer paper, computer, and inkjet printer)

Coordinating cotton embroidery floss

Embellishments to decorate bag, such as buttons, bows, and rosebud trims

Hot glue and hot-glue gun

Favors to fill bag

It's a Boy! or It's a Girl! tag and curling ribbon (optional)

WHAT YOU DO

1. To embellish one tote bag, cut a 5-inch-square piece of the print fabric.

2. Apply the fusible web onto the piece of fabric (see Fusible Web Appliqué, page 12), then cut the fabric piece down to approximately 4 x 3¾ inches using pinking shears, and fuse it onto the center of the bag.

3. Follow the manufacturer's instructions for the photo transfer paper to transfer the photo onto the natural cotton fabric, then trim around the photo with pinking shears. (See page 16 for more on using photo transfers.)

4. Baste the photo onto the center of the fused fabric piece, then straight stitch around the photo using two strands of matching floss.

5. Hot glue (or stitch) the decorative trims onto the bag as desired.

6. Fill the bag with the favors, and—for the final touch—tie an "It's a Boy!" or "It's a Girl" tag onto the handle with curling ribbon.

Chenille Memory Album

An ordinary, store-bought memory album becomes an enchanting keepsake when embellished with a collage of sweet mementos. The fun begins by transferring a favorite photo onto fabric. The photo and a stamped footprint are then stitched onto a chenille cover along with some fabric patches, recycled denim belt loops, and other crafty trims. An embroidered name tag adds a cute finishing touch.

A diaper bag is a necessity for a new mom, but those store-bought varieties can be so boring. For just a few dollars, you can dress up a plain canvas tote bag with a colorful cotton print and your precious tot's photo. Canvas totes come in a variety of sizes, so you can choose the one that's right for you. The bag can also be used in the nursery to store toys or changing necessities.

WHAT YOU NEED

Basic materials, tools, and equipment (page 17)

Piece of floral print fabric, 12 x 12 inches

Fusible web

Natural cotton canvas tote bag, 13½ x 13½ inches

Fabric printed photo, 5¾ x 7¾ inches (Scrap of heavyweight natural cotton fabric; digital photo, 5 x 7 inches; photo transfer paper, computer, and inkjet printer)

Coordinating cotton embroidery floss

Pink pom-pom trim (enough to fit around the top of the bag), 1 inch wide

2 pieces of jumbo pink chenille rickrack (to fit along the length of the handles of the bag)

4 pieces of pink ribbon, each ⅝ x 14 inches

2 pink chick buttons

4 pink ribbon flowers with pearl centers, each 1½ inches wide

WHAT YOU DO

1. Apply the fusible web to the 12 x 12-inch piece of fabric (see Fusible Web Appliqué, page 12), then use pinking shears to trim the fabric until it's 11 inches square.

2. Fuse the fabric square onto the center of the bag.

3. Follow the manufacturer's instructions for the photo transfer paper to transfer the photo onto the piece of natural cotton fabric, then trim around the photo with pinking shears to create a border. (See page 16 for more on using photo transfers.)

4. Baste the photo onto the center of the fused fabric piece, then sew a running stitch around the edge of the photo using three strands of coordinating floss.

5. Cut a piece of the pink pom-pom trim that's long enough to fit around the top of the bag, then stitch the trim onto the bag.

6. Cut two pieces of the pink rickrack trim that are long enough to fit along the length of the handles of the bag, then stitch the trim onto the handles.

7. Tie four bows with the pink ribbon, then stitch each of the bows onto the ends of the two handles.

8. Stitch the pink chick buttons onto the two front bows.

9. Stitch the four pink ribbon flowers onto each corner of the photo.

Baby's First Year Soft Keepsake Book

Capture the magical memories of that first year with this oh-so-soft keepsake book. Embellish the pages with favorite photos, Baby's footprints, and other tiny treasures or mementos. Simple embroidery stitches are a fun way to add dates, titles, and captions to your photos and to journal those special thoughts and sentiments.

WHAT YOU NEED

Basic materials, tools, and equipment (page 17)

Bear and pocket templates (page 134)

Scraps of tan and cream plush felt

Scraps of black and cream felt

6 pieces of cream felt, 8 x 8 inches

Cotton embroidery floss in dark brown, black, and pale green (or color to match bows)

3 pieces of pale green ribbon, each ⅛ x 9 inches

Fabric printed photos, 5¼ x 4¼ inches and 3 x 3½ inches (Scraps of heavyweight natural cotton fabric; digital photos, 5 x 4 inches and 2¾ x 3¼ inches; photo transfer paper, computer, and inkjet printer)

Stamped baby footprints (Scraps of heavyweight natural cotton fabric, petroleum jelly, and child-safe black inkpad)

5¼ inches of scalloped felt or ribbon trim, 1¾ inches wide (optional for decorating pocket)

WHAT YOU DO

To make the cover page:

1. Use the bear template on page 134 to trace and cut out the bear head from the tan plush felt, the muzzle from the cream plush felt, and the nose from the black felt.

2. Baste the bear onto one of the square felt pieces, then blanket-stitch around the head and muzzle, using two strands of the dark brown floss. Stitch two black French knots for the eyes.

3. Stitch around the nose to secure it, using two strands of the black floss, then backstitch a small line running down the center of the nose. Add a tiny black French knot at the bottom of the stitched line for the mouth.

4. Trace "My First Year" (or your desired title), then backstitch it using two strands of the brown floss. Tie a bow with one piece of the pale green ribbon and stitch it onto the bottom of the bear.

Page Idea #1: Add a Photo

5. Follow the manufacturer's instructions for the photo transfer paper to transfer the 5 x 4-inch photo onto a piece of the natural cotton fabric, then trim around the photo with pinking shears to create a small border. (See page 16 for more on using photo transfers.)

6. Baste the photo onto one of the felt squares, then straight stitch around the photo using two strands of the pale green floss. Tie a bow with another piece of the pale green ribbon, and stitch it onto the bottom center of the photo.

Page Idea #2: Add Stamped Baby Footprints

7. To make the footprints, cover the bottom of Baby's feet with a light coat of petroleum jelly. Press Baby's feet firmly onto the inkpad, then directly onto the scrap pieces of natural cotton fabric. Trim

around the footprints with pinking shears, and let the pieces dry. (Note: Remove ink immediately from Baby's feet.)

8. Baste the two footprints, overlapping one another, onto one of the felt squares, then straight stitch around the footprints using two strands of the pale green floss. Backstitch Baby's age using two strands of the brown floss.

Page Idea #3: Add a Caption and a Photo

9. Follow steps 5 and 6 using the 2¾ x 3¼-inch photo. Instead of adding a bow, backstitch a cute caption to capture the theme of the photo. Ideas include: "I Can Crawl," "My First Bath," "Mommy and Me," "Nap Time," and "My Favorite Toy."

Page Idea #4: Add a Keepsake Pocket

10. Use the pocket template on page 134 to trace and cut out a pocket shape from a scrap of the cream felt. For added interest, stitch a piece of scalloped felt, some ribbon trim, or a bow onto the top of the pocket.

11. Blanket-stitch along the top straight edge of the pocket (where the pocket will remain open), using two strands of the brown floss. (You will complete the blanket stitch around the pocket in the next step.)

12. Pin the pocket onto another one of the felt squares, then continue to blanket-stitch around the pocket so that the stitches join the ones already in place along the top straight edge.

13. Tuck a favorite keepsake into the pocket—a lock of Baby's hair, a birth announcement, hospital bracelet, or small toy.

To assemble the book:

14. Pin the bear cover page to another page of your choice (I chose the larger single photo) wrong sides together, then pin two more of the pages (I chose the footprints and the smaller "I can crawl!" photo) wrong sides together. Pin the final page (mine is the keepsake pocket) onto the remaining blank felt square (the blank square will be the back cover of the book).

15. Refer to steps 14 to 17 on page 106 to finish the book, substituting the pale green floss for the aqua blue floss.

tip

If you don't have a digital camera or a scanner, you can have your regular print film burned onto a disc or CD at your local photo processing center.

Templates

Sweet Dreams Bunny Nursery Accent and Pillow
page 22

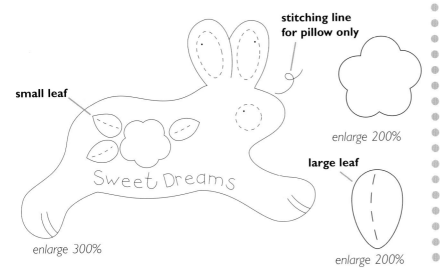

stitching line for pillow only

small leaf

large leaf

Sweet Dreams

enlarge 300%

enlarge 200%

enlarge 200%

Busy Bee Slippers
page 54

actual size

Tooth Fairy Pillow
page 32

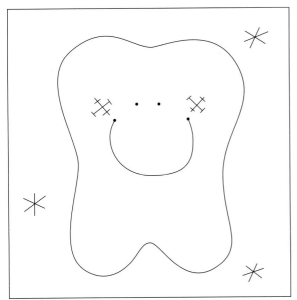

enlarge 200%

Counting Sheep Pillow and Wall Quilt
page 26

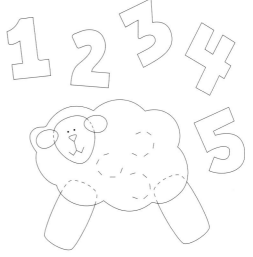

enlarge 300%

Goodnight Moon Crib Blanket and Mobile   page 34

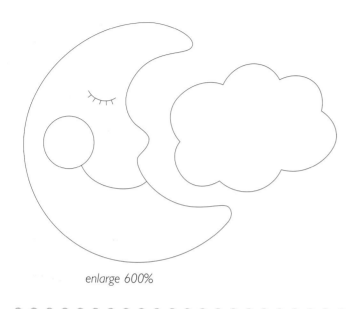

enlarge 600%

Designer Denim Bibs
page 51

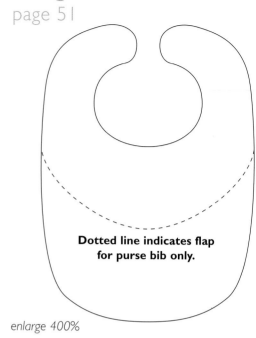

Dotted line indicates flap for purse bib only.

enlarge 400%

Snuggle Bug Crib Blanket   page 40

enlarge 300%

enlarge 200%

Lullaby Lambs Door Hanger page 42

enlarge 200%

Frog Pond Rug
page 30

enlarge 400%

Fleecy Friends Bibs page 56

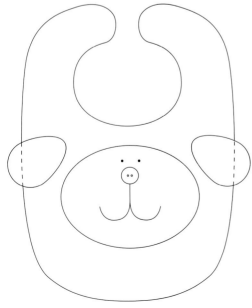

enlarge 400%

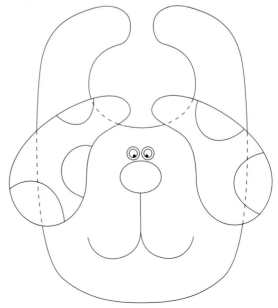

enlarge 400%

See Ya Later Alligator Scarf and Mittens   page 59

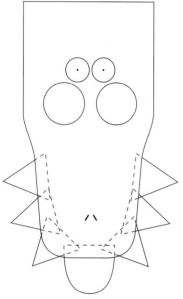

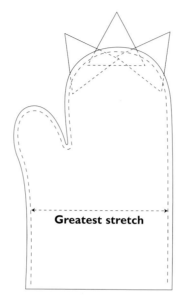

Greatest stretch

enlarge 400%

enlarge 300%

Cupcake Cutie Blanket, Apron, and Favor Bags   page 72

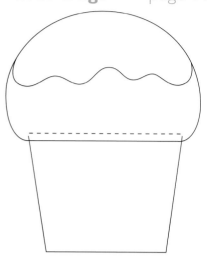

for Blanket, enlarge 500%
for Apron, enlarge 425%
for Favor Bags, enlarge 200%

Chic Kitty Purse and Scarf   page 62

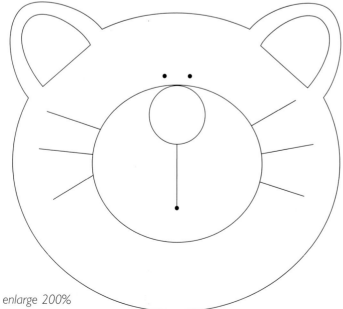

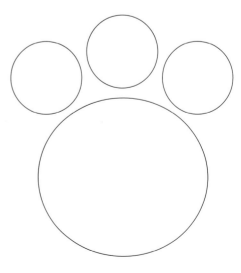

enlarge 200%

enlarge 200%

Chenille Snuggle Bunny and Mini Quilt   page 68

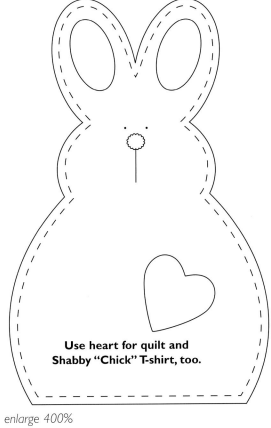

Use heart for quilt and Shabby "Chick" T-shirt, too.

enlarge 400%

Pocket Bunny Activity Blanket
page 101

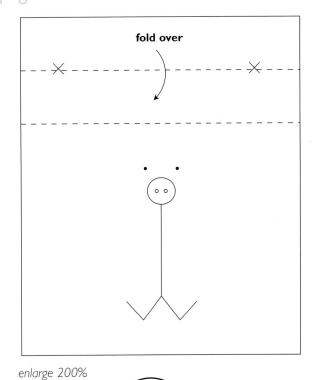

fold over

enlarge 200%

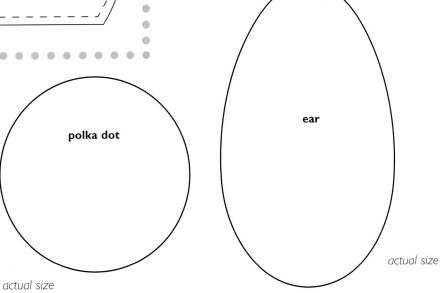

polka dot

actual size

ear

actual size

Dirty Duds Cow Laundry Bag page 82

casing

enlarge 650%

Giraffe Cuddle Blanket page ?

enlarge 600%

Ribbit Frog Rattle
page 96

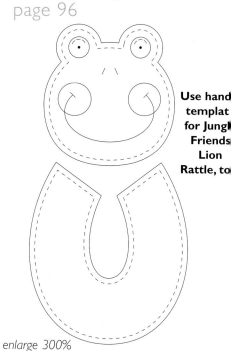

Use hand
templat
for Jung
Friends
Lion
Rattle, to

Wiggly Worm Play Pal
page 94

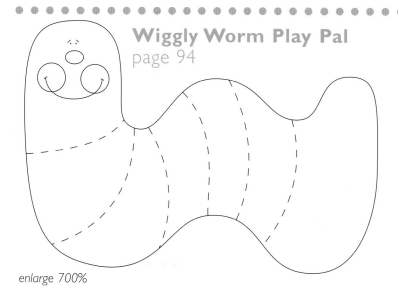

enlarge 700%

enlarge 300%

Ocean Friends Activity Mat

page 88

enlarge 500%

Jungle Friends Pacifier Pals, Puppets, and Rattle

page 91

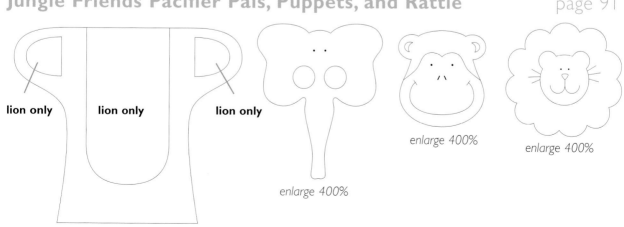

lion only   **lion only**   **lion only**

enlarge 400%

enlarge 400%

enlarge 400%

enlarge 400%

What's in My Pocket? Activity Book page 104

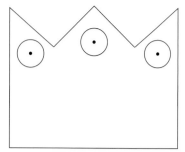

enlarge 200%

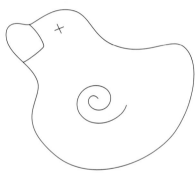

enlarge 200%

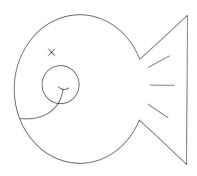

enlarge 200%

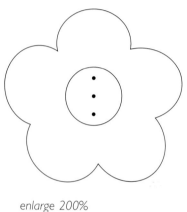

enlarge 200%

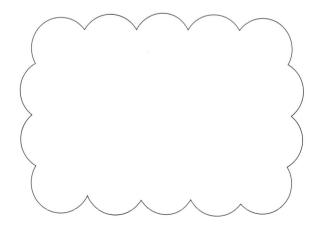

enlarge 200%

Baby's First Year Soft Keepsake Book
page 124

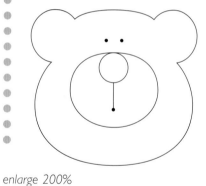

enlarge 200%

Keepsake Birth Pillow page 112

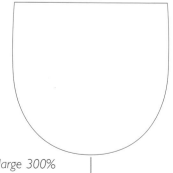

enlarge 400%

enlarge 300%

(Use for What's in My Pocket? Activity Book, too.)

Sweet Treats Counting Book   page 107

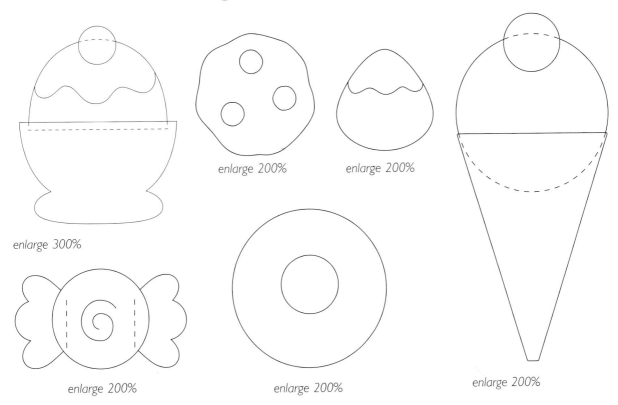

enlarge 200%

enlarge 200%

enlarge 300%

enlarge 200%

enlarge 200%

enlarge 200%

Barnyard Buddy Blocks   page 98

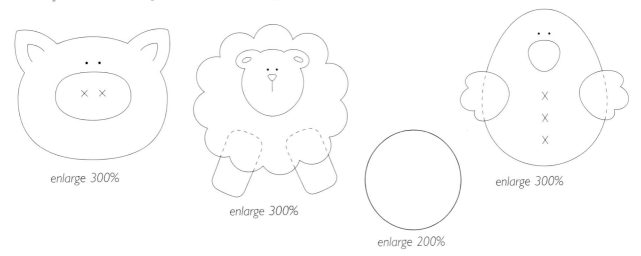

enlarge 300%

enlarge 300%

enlarge 300%

enlarge 200%

Acknowledgments

First and foremost, I would like to thank my special cousin, Gay Ryan, for so generously offering her time, talent, creativity and support throughout this entire process. And to her sweet Kali, thanks for resisting the temptation to "strut your stuff" on the table during our sewing sessions.

I must also extend my sincere appreciation to Phyllis Johnson and all the great gals at Crazy Ladies Fabrics, for your expertise and for all of the helpful tips and suggestions. You "crazy ladies" make even the most technical aspects of writing a book so much fun!

Special thanks to my wonderful editor, Kathy Sheldon, senior editor Paige Gilchrist, assistant editor Julie Hale, and all the fine folks at Lark, Sterling, and Chapelle for granting me this amazing opportunity. The book design is absolutely stunning and for that I must thank art director Dana Irwin, associate Lance Wille, and photographer John Widman.

For the charming photos used in the image transfer projects, I thank Jan Hall-Bosma, a very talented photographer and wonderful lady who has such a kind and giving spirit. And let's not forget those "picture-perfect" tots: Jane Marie, Jasper, Josie, Julianna, Kendal, Lilyan Alivea Grace, Lillyan Violet, Loren, Oona, Ryan, Scarlet, Solomon, Sophia, Tazé, Tazé's brother, Thalia, and Walker Shane for inspiring me with those sweet cheeks and precious poses. And thanks also to your parents for allowing me to share these magical memories.

As always, I thank my husband, Tom, and Pops, Laurie, Auntie Mary, Michael, and Karen for your continued encouragement and support.

This book is dedicated to my crafty cousins, Ellen and Gay, and their spoiled brat kitties.

Metric Conversion Chart

INCHES	METRIC (MM/CM)	INCHES	METRIC (MM/CM)	INCHES	METRIC (MM/CM)	INCHES	METRIC (MM/CM)
1/8	3 mm	1½	3.8 cm	9	22.9 cm	16½	41.9 cm
3/16	5 mm	2	5 cm	9½	24.1 cm	17	43.2 cm
1/4	6 mm	2½	6.4 cm	10	25.4 cm	17½	44.5 cm
5/16	8 mm	3	7.6 cm	10½	26.7 cm	18	45.7 cm
3/8	9.5 mm	3½	8.9 cm	11	27.9 cm	18½	47 cm
7/16	1.1 cm	4	10.2 cm	11½	29.2 cm	19	48.3 cm
1/2	1.3 cm	4½	11.4 cm	12	30.5 cm	19½	49.5 cm
9/16	1.4 cm	5	12.7 cm	12½	31.8 cm	20	50.8 cm
5/8	1.6 cm	5½	14 cm	13	33 cm	20½	52 cm
11/16	1.7 cm	6	15.2 cm	13½	34.3 cm	21	53.3 cm
3/4	1.9 cm	6½	16.5 cm	14	35.6 cm	21½	54.6 cm
13/16	2.1 cm	7	17.8 cm	14½	36.8 cm	22	55 cm
7/8	2.2 cm	7½	19 cm	15	38.1 cm	22½	57.2 cm
15/16	2.4 cm	8	20.3 cm	15½	39.4 cm	23	58.4 cm
1	2.5 cm	8½	21.6 cm	16	40.6 cm	24	61 cm

Index

Baby's First Year Soft Keepsake Book   124

Barnyard Buddy Blocks   98

Basics   8

Bath-Time Buddies Hooded Bath Towel   80

Bedtime Buddies Crib Mobile   37

Busy Bee Slippers   54

Chenille Memory Album   121

Chenille Snuggle Bunny and Mini Quilt   68

Chic Kitty Purse and Scarf   62

Counting Sheep Pillow and Wall Quilt   26

Cupcake Cutie Blanket, Apron, and Favor Bags   72

Cute as a Button Critter Cap   46

Designer Denim Bibs   51

Dirty Duds Cow Laundry Bag   82

Embroidery techniques   14

Fabric   9

Fleecy Friends Bibs   56

Frog Pond Rug   30

Fusible web   12

Giraffe Cuddle Blanket   78

Goodnight Moon Crib Blanket and Mobile   34

Jungle Friends Pacifier Pals, Puppets, and Rattle   91

Keepsake Birth Pillow   112

Keepsake Memory Quilt and Pillow   116

Lullaby Lambs (Baby Sleeping) Door Hanger   42

Metric Conversion Chart   137

Mini Jean Pocket Purse   114

Ocean Friends Activity Mat   88

Photo transfer   16

Pocket Bunny Activity Blanket   101

Ribbit Frog Rattle   96

Rub-a-Dub-Dub Bath Bag   84

See Ya Later Alligator Scarf and Mittens   59

Seam Allowances   11

Shabby Chick Hanger, T-Shirt, Booties, and Socks   48

Snuggle Bug Crib Blanket   40

Special Delivery Tote Bags   120

Spring Blossom Diaper Bag   122

Stitch guide   15

Sweet Dreams Bunny Nursery Accent and Pillow   22

Sweet Treats Counting Book   107

Templates   127

Tooth Fairy Pillow   32

"What's in My Pocket?" Activity Book   104

Wiggly Worm Play Pal   94